STOP
OVERTHINKING

Declutter Your Mind, Master Your Emotions, and
Eliminate Negative Thinking

LUCAS BAILEY

© **Copyright 2023 - All rights reserved.**

The content contained within this book may not be reproduced, duplicated, or transmitted without direct written permission from the author or the publisher.

Under no circumstances will any blame or legal responsibility be held against the publisher, or author, for any damages, reparation, or monetary loss due to the information contained within this book, either directly or indirectly.

Legal Notice:

This book is copyright protected. It is only for personal use. You cannot amend, distribute, sell, use, quote or paraphrase any part, or the content within this book, without the consent of the author or publisher.

Disclaimer Notice:

Please note the information contained within this document is for educational and entertainment purposes only. All effort has been executed to present accurate, up to date, reliable, complete information. No warranties of any kind are declared or implied. Readers acknowledge that the author is not engaged in the rendering of legal, financial, medical or professional advice. The content within this book has been derived from various sources. Please consult a licensed professional before attempting any techniques outlined in this book.

By reading this document, the reader agrees that under no circumstances is the author responsible for any losses, direct or indirect, that are incurred as a result of the use of the information contained within this document, including, but not limited to, errors, omissions, or inaccuracies.

Your FREE Bonuses

Download the following short form eBooks as a free supplement to your learning.

Bonus 1:

7 Ideas to Help You

Stop Caring What Everyone Thinks

Discover How to:

- Do what you do without a second thought
- Move on quickly
- Understand that with practice it gets easier
- … and more

Bonus 2:
8 Techniques for Making Quick Decisions

Discover:

- Useful tips for avoiding indecision
- Short hacks to avoid delaying
- How sticking to your values moves you forward
- ... and more

Bonus 3:
9 Ways to Stop Sabotaging Yourself!

Discover:

- How to focus on goals
- How to visualize positive outcomes
- How to stop fearing failure & build self-esteem
- … and more

To download your 3 free bonuses:

7 Ideas to Help You
Stop Caring What Everyone Thinks

8 Techniques for Making Quick Decisions

9 Ways to Stop Sabotaging Yourself!

Scan the QR code above with the camara function
on your cell phone and click the link.

"Once you realize you deserve a bright future, letting go of your dark past is the best choice you will ever make."

- ROY T. BENNETT

Contents

	Introduction	1
Chapter 1	**The Science of Overthinking**	5
Chapter 2	**First Steps to Decluttering Your Mind**	29
Chapter 3	**Forgiving Past You So Present You Can Invest in Future You**	40
Chapter 4	**Overthinking and Our Relationships**	59
Chapter 5	**Mastering Your Emotions**	79
Chapter 6	**Setting Yourself Up for Self-Growth**	104
Chapter 7	**Managing the Growing Pains of Risk**	119
Chapter 8	**Staying Motivated and Accountable**	134
	Conclusion	148
	References	151

STOP
OVERTHINKING

INTRODUCTION

We find that often, we are our own worst enemies. There might be a little voice in your head that will go over every way you can fail in stunning detail. This voice is illogical and harmful, but ultimately a part of us. For some people, this voice is louder than it is for others. These are the overthinkers of the world. While overthinking can be spun into a good thing, it is a lead weight wrapped around our ankles during our daily lives, or worse—when we have the audacity to want to leave our comfort zone.

We think of this voice as our friend, our protector from our baser instincts and the dangers of the world, there to talk us out of our "dumber" ideas. In reality, overthinking has probably held you back more than it has helped you. How often have you talked yourself out of doing something fun because you were afraid of looking silly? How many missed chances have you had because you did not socially and professionally put yourself out there?

How many things have you quit because that voice told you that you were no good and you should just give up and save a few bucks? Your voice of reason and that little gremlin that only exists to tell you how much you suck are two wildly different things.

To reach your full potential, you need to let those doubts go. You will only take risks, finish projects, or create new connections if you are the first person telling yourself that you will succeed. This is not purely a mental journey. Several concrete steps you can take in your life will reduce the noise in your head and focus on the things that really matter. Maladaptive emotions bog down our internal and external lives, and way too many choices in our lives, from what we study to which one of fifty breakfast cereals we want to buy this week and how best to construct a critical email. It's no wonder we are so exhausted.

It should be noted, however, that some issues with overthinking require intervention from a specialist.

Everyone deserves to pursue their goals without someone (even if it's themselves) discouraging it. We can quiet that voice and replace it with more productive thoughts through mindfulness, reframing, and self-care. Once you understand your brain and thought patterns, you can turn the tide and live a life of growth and positivity.

INTRODUCTION

Overthinking Is Not Always a Bad Thing

Our noisy brains can be a gift in certain situations, and you should not dismiss every thought in your head as being a negative Nancy. While the sheer volume of your thoughts can be an issue, how you react to negativity is also essential. There is such a thing as toxic positivity, which can be just as unhelpful as rumination. Accepting things at face value and not questioning things can leave you with blind spots, and you can end up in a deeper hole than you would have if you had just put a bit more thought in.

Being vigilant of weak points is a legitimate skill that not everyone has. You can use this insight to plan your everyday life or to troubleshoot issues when they come up. Lateral thinking will give you a massive advantage in this world. This ability to think outside the box is an asset. Your solutions can be more creative, and you can often see things before everyone else. You are also less likely to let something go that can become a potential fire, since you can see the consequences clearly as opposed to someone that can only think in the present moment.

You are also more likely to be self-aware and introspective because you think about what you do and how it affects others (Sedgwick et al., 2019). If you pause and let yourself reflect, you might be able to get ahead of a person's emotions. You can clarify or apologize for a misstep before the other person can even register that you might have been dismissive or confusing. You also might have an amazing sense of humor. Since you probably have a pretty decent recall of things you actually like and have the ability to be light on your feet during a conversation, you might think of zingers, pop culture references, and weird facts on the fly. People with ADHD report that this is a positive side effect of their condition (Cootey, 2019). Since they sometimes have trouble bonding emotionally with people immediately, they make them laugh as an in. While being funny is not enough to form a long-term connection, it is a good way to make people like you. This helps people give you grace when the more troublesome parts of your overthinking rear their ugly heads.

Finally, if you have picked up this book, you have probably been dealing with the curse of a brain that goes a mile a minute since you were a kid. You have probably already found tricks to deal with things and might find that some parts of this book seem familiar. You already have a level of resilience that most people cannot even fathom. If you had to switch brains with someone who seems infuriatingly easygoing, they would probably be in the fetal position in an hour. You are likely already a hard worker and can rise to the occasion when the situation demands. You just need to figure out how to make your brain work with the world that is not the kindest to overthinkers.

THE SCIENCE OF OVERTHINKING

"The greatest freedom is to be free of our own mind."

- OSHO

Maria has let her apartment spiral out of control. She had been dealing with depression the entire winter, and it took all of her energy to just function and go to work. Her apartment was wholly neglected. Now that the fog has lifted, she faces the Herculean task that awaits her. She doesn't have much choice in the matter, her parents are coming over in two days, and she needs her apartment fit for her mother's approval.

She tried to decide where to start. The bathroom seemed logical, but she backed off when she thought about the active germs, dried spit, and fumes of cleaning products. Next was her bedroom. Her bedding knotted together in a ball and dirty laundry on every surface looked impossible. Maybe the kitchen? Nope. There were tiny flies around her sink, and she realized that she had not taken out the trash in weeks. She thought she saw a maggot peeking out of the lid and ran out. How about the living room? No, the furniture needed to be moved so she could get to the colony of dust bunnies underneath, her couch needed vacuuming, and every surface needed to be disinfected.

Maria did rounds in her apartment, attempting to start, only to be disgusted or distracted by another task. It had been an hour, and she had made no progress. Then an idea popped into her head; she could go online and look at the content to inspire her into cleaning mode. An hour later, she had done forty-five minutes of research on the French Revolution, then finally fifteen minutes of cleaning research. She concluded she needed to go to the store to buy a specific cleaner, some rags, and a scrubber to tackle the big job. Plus, the purchase might motivate her. Another hour later, she returned with the rags, chips, a can of Red Bull, and no cleaner and scrubber. Maria got frustrated and took a fifteen-minute break to scroll on TikTok. Four hours later, she realized she had accomplished nothing.

This wasn't working, and Maria didn't know what to do. The clock was ticking, and she had to think of something. Negative thoughts hounded her:

- *How could you let things get this bad?*
- *You are lazy.*
- *You are disgusting.*

- *Your parents are going to be mortified when they see this.*
- *They will tell all the relatives they have a pig instead of a daughter.*
- *You have probably accidentally eaten a maggot this winter.*
- *What kind of an adult are you?*
- *You are pathetic.*
- *Why bother?*

Every time Maria tried to think of a plan, her negativity–fueled by Red Bull and shame–overpowered the logical side of her brain. An overwhelming sense of dread effectively froze her. Something had to change.

What is Overthinking?

At first blush, our overthinking sounds like the voice of reason in our heads, an angel that keeps us in line and has our best interests at heart. However, it is often the opposite. A better word for overthinking used in the scientific community is *rumination*. This is a single-minded attempt to cope by grasping negative emotions and potential consequences. A person ruminating on a job interview probably thinks:

- *I'm not going to get the job.*

- *I will look so dumb they will probably blacklist me from the industry.*
- *If I don't nail this, I won't be able to pay rent, I'll be homeless, and starve to death under a bridge.*

This is in contrast to a *distraction,* which is the mind's attempt to steer away from uncomfortable thoughts. One doubles down on the negativity; the other tries to avoid it entirely. A distracted person will most likely avoid prepping for the interview by staying in bed and watching YouTube videos on sticky bun recipes. People develop these two different coping mechanisms in the face of resistance. It is not a form of cowardice, laziness, or denial; it is simply how people are *made* through trauma, neurodivergence, or chronic stress. It is so ingrained that we start to see that nagging voice as a friend; after all, we know ourselves best, and that voice wouldn't exist if we didn't need it. We need to recognize the difference between natural intuition, self-reflection, and overthinking. The first two are born of life experience and benefit us in the long run. Rumination is mentally harmful, exacerbates depressive symptoms, and is even an indicator of suicidality.

Overthinking is often a response to a lack of control. We are the center of our universe; the idea that we are at the mercy of the whims of strangers, or the unpredictability of nature is difficult to fathom. It is why regions more likely to suffer natural disasters tend to be more religious and emphasize ritual, and athletes develop superstitions.

These tangible acts can make people feel safe in a world that can snuff out their hopes and dreams without blinking. Feeling small can lead to lower self-esteem, which also breeds rumination. Everything you do is wrong, you will never be truly ready, and staying in your comfort zone is safer. It is a cruel cycle of overthinking, making mistakes, being "proven right" in failure, and consequently retreating to safety. It is a cycle that will doom you to a life where you never take a single chance or challenge yourself.

Rumination and neurodivergence can be a chicken or egg conundrum. Did a need to overthink turn into generalized anxiety? Or are people who are predisposed to anxiety also just prone to overthinking? Whichever came first doesn't change the fact that they feed into each other. Disorders include:

- Generalized anxiety
- Social anxiety
- Depression
- Post-Traumatic Stress Disorder (PTSD)
- Attention Deficit Hyperactivity Disorder (ADHD)
- Obsessive Compulsive Disorder (OCD)
- Autism

Bizarrely enough, rumination and neurodivergence have been normalized and even trivialized in our society. People brush off symptoms as simple jitters or signs that someone needs to "man up" or stop being spoiled. It shouldn't need to be said, but getting diarrhea every time you had a math test because the stress was wreaking havoc on your digestive system is not normal. Figuring out coping mechanisms and even seeking professional help, if you can access them, is a form of self-care everyone is entitled to.

There is a reason that therapy for these disorders is often recommended in conjunction with medication. Correcting a chemical imbalance is often insufficient; a person must combat self-deprecating attitudes. Negative thoughts are not a choice; they can be the brain's default mode for challenging situations. Think of a person's stress response as a car alarm. For some models, it takes a pretty big bump to trigger the obnoxious alarm; for others, a light tap will wake up a neighborhood at 3 a.m. Despite the human nervous system being a marvel of biology, our fight or flight reaction can be dirt simple. A person fired on a Friday may jump every time they receive an email from their boss on a Friday going forward. They may fear all dogs after getting bitten by a single dog in childhood. They may avoid public speaking for the rest of their lives after a poor performance in their elementary school play. These thoughts may seem like a shotgun approach to very specific set of circumstances, but to the person affected, they are the only way they know how to protect themselves.

Recognizing Harmful Thought Patterns

The first step to stop overthinking is to recognize how these thought patterns present in you. There are several types of "cognitive distortions", or how our brain warps situations to feed our anxieties. This level of rumination is not based on objective evidence and seems silly when laid out. Ironically, these distortions become self-fulfilling prophecies. It is not taking a chance that makes a person crash and burn; it is priming themselves for disaster in the first place (Rapee & Heimberg, 1997).

Fortune Telling

The "fortune teller phenomenon" is when a person decides how a situation will turn out right off the bat. Often, it is the worst-case scenario. A person has already decided they will be stood up for a date because they have experienced it in the past. The person on the other end could have been the most attentive texter, funny, charming, and confirmed their meetup. But, since the overthinker has been burned in the past, they are setting themselves up for disappointment so at least surprise won't be on their list of emotions felt. If anything, feeling good about another person and getting giddy with anticipation might make this worse—now there is something to lose. A subset of this distortion is *mind reading*. We tend to guess a person's opinion of us based on a brief interaction and maybe even hearsay. If you are meeting someone and they arch their eyebrow weirdly at a comment you made or appear icy, you may conclude that you made a poor first impression and that they hate you. It is an unfortunate distortion that can rob a person of good anticipatory feelings at best and sabotage them at worst (Cuzzone, 2020).

Magical Thinking

While this can be adaptive, "magical thinking" can warp into a cognitive distortion depending on the circumstances. Developing a good luck ritual to calm your nerves or look for positive signs from the universe is harmless and can even be beneficial, no matter how illogical it might sound. This is your superstitious person who believes they will have a bad day because they forgot to wear their lucky socks. Humans love control, which is rarely afforded to us, so we compensate in other ways to at least *feel* like we are in control (Gomez, 2022).

All or Nothing Thinking

If you have ever seen someone cry in school over an 85% on a test, then you know exactly what this is. These are the perfectionists who can only see the world in win or lose, black or white. However, since most of us are down on ourselves, we tend to default to nothing more often than not. A manager can give this person a performance review that is 95% adoration but point out that they could send emails out more promptly. The all or nothing thinker will pirouette into thoughts of failure, fear of getting fired, or paranoia that their supervisors secretly hate them. It can make a person sensitive to criticism and setbacks and stall the process rather than aid it (Carucci, 2022).

Discounting Positives

This is the song of pessimists and those that struggle with self-esteem. This is all or nothing thinking if the "all" was replaced with more "nothing". Instead of rose-tinted glasses, this person is subjected to shit-covered goggles and is either blind to or completely unable to accept praise. This can manifest itself in what is widely known as "imposter syndrome". No matter how high a person climbs and what they achieve, they never feel like they belong. Instead of being smart, they are "a hard worker who is good at taking tests." If they get a job, they chalk it up to tricking everyone into thinking they are competent. The "imposter" will live in fear that the jig will be up one day when they make a fatal error and expose themselves as the dummy that should have never been allowed in. This is not humility; this is a cascade of unearned shame that makes people see themselves as failures. If people do not see themselves as worthy of success, they will never take chances and often remain invisible to avoid scrutiny (Palma, 2021).

Personalization

This is centering every problem around yourself, whether it is in your control or not. If a group project fails, it's because of you; you weren't careful enough, didn't watch the team, and didn't come up with better ideas. The project could have failed due to someone else's mistakes or a team-wide breakdown or a whole slew of factors. This behavior often emerges in childhood. If your mother is angry for any reason, you assume that you are the cause or are responsible for fixing it. You may start obsessively cleaning the house and be on your best behavior in an effort to appease a hurricane of emotions. Once again, it is a desperate grasp for control.

Personalization can be born from many things, including unstable homes where a child learns to walk on eggshells around a parent with an explosive temper. They fight and claw their way into a peaceful existence despite having no control over the other person. Sometimes their attempts work, but most times, it is fruitless, yet they keep trying (Joy, 2022).

Magnification

This is the tendency to put a lot of importance on a minute detail to justify one's opinion. This can happen a lot on dating profiles. If a woman sees a man in a Star Wars shirt, she might take him for an insufferable nerd who could not possibly have anything in common with her instead of a casual fan. In one photo, a man can see a woman wearing red lipstick and think she has a vain personality or is insecure without much makeup. This is a form of self-sabotage as we find ourselves practically seeking reasons not to engage with other people or tasks (Star, n.d.-a). At worst, it can morph into...

Catastrophizing

This severe cognitive distortion makes a person's life feel like a minefield. It can be borne of trauma or general anxiety over a particular pain point in someone's life.

- A graduate student desperate for their boss's approval may get a stomach ache every time she interacts with their supervisor because they "know" they will be kicked out of the program.
- A person with a headache may start planning their funeral because they "know" they have brain cancer.
- A woman second guesses going on a date because she is "convinced" there is a chance the man may murder her and dump her in the river.

Every thought is the worst-case scenario, and while some of these examples sound funny, it is an exhausting way to live. While they may seem illogical, it makes perfect sense to a catastrophizer because they are living their life planning around and expecting the worst (Fletcher, 2022). For some reason, optimism can be seen as a weakness in humans, especially overthinkers. Not only are you in a tough place, but the idea that life somehow duped you into having a positive mindset makes it worse.

When I choose to see the good side of things, I'm not being naive. It is strategic and necessary. It's how I learned to survive through everything.

- Everything Everywhere All at Once

Let's say two people need to see a doctor for a headache and are told by their primary doctors to see a specialist. One is taking the whole thing in their stride, and while the thought of something serious crosses his mind, he looks at the facts and determines it's probably nothing. Another man is convinced that he has a brain tumor. It takes a month for each man to be seen by a specialist. While the first man continues to live his life, the other man is feverishly searching WebMD and spiraling into morbid thoughts. A week before his visit, he thinks about drafting a will and picking out a casket.

Both these men are fine, but the question is who is better off? Just because the outcome was the same, does not mean that this experience did not have a profoundly negative effect on one of them. The first man might take this whole experience as a lesson to watch his blood pressure, but ultimately comes out unscathed. The catastrophizer just saw his life flash before his eyes and has spent an entire month chronically stressed. His hormones are out of whack, his sleep has suffered, and he will always remember how scared he was whenever he has a headache. Subconsciously, he might avoid going to the doctor in the future. There is no safety in catastrophizing; there is only fear and despair.

Overgeneralization

This distortion leads to assumptions that can encompass many topics despite little evidence (Michael, 2022). For example, suppose a person becomes discouraged at a watercolor class. In that case, they might assume they are bad at all art and give up the hobby altogether despite only trying one medium. This need to make sweeping assumptions keeps a person from trying different tactics. This particular distortion can harm others as well. A man who picks up the slack for a woman at one job may now not trust any woman he encounters in the workplace. To him, it's not that this one particular woman was a terrible employee; now he sees all women as a professional burden. Being caught in the snare of a cognitive distortion is not always your fault, but it is your responsibility to recognize and deal with it.

Recognizing Triggers

While these thoughts are integrated into our brains, they tend to flare up in the face of specific triggers that can be internal or external. External triggers include:

- acute stress

- unpredictability/uncertainty
    - interacting with people
    - big life changes
- PTSD or trauma
- lack of control
- risk
    - reputation
    - financial

We are always seeking the correct answer to solve any issue our environment can throw our way despite only having our perspectives to go off of. Sudden stressors are ubiquitous in us all at one point or another. A person who feels a lump on their body may jump to a vision of their funeral. It is difficult to see any hope, which can exacerbate morbid conclusions and lead to more panic. This is when snap decisions, emotional volatility, and desperation lead us to do things we regret, perpetuating the cycle.

Another trigger is unpredictability and ambiguity, specifically around dealing with others and significant life changes. We want people to like us and be impressed by us. Since we can't read minds, we will re-examine every interaction we have with new people leading to a less-than-charitable analysis of our social skills. This is magnified when the other person is in a position of power, like a manager or a celebrity. Looking through a celebrity's social media and seeing an army of people competing for attention by giving the best compliments is proof of this. This trigger can turn a reasonable person into a doormat with no self-respect.

Overthinking significant life changes can be a baffling experience. They can arise from losing a job or coming down with a chronic illness, but they can also occur from good things like getting pregnant after years of trying, getting a new job, or moving somewhere new. You might have been working for years towards a specific goal, and when you finally get it–you are scared shitless. The thought of now having to prove yourself (even though you already did) and being thrust into a new environment is terrifying, and it can rob you of the joy of what should be one of the happiest moments of your year, if not your life. Your life was one way, and you were used to that, even if you weren't pleased. Now that comfort is gone, you need to deal with the consequences of your success.

One of the final triggers is the introduction of risk. Whether reputation or money, these can rattle the cage of even the most seasoned professionals. Extensive talks in front of movers and shakers of the industry, having to buy a house and being tied to a mortgage for thirty years, or putting money down to get an education can suddenly stop the momentum. You may now try and justify why you don't need to take that risk.

Internal triggers include:

- indecision brought on by too many choices
- perfectionism
- vulnerability

As we have learned from dating apps and long menus, too many choices can be a burden. Despite most situations having more than one correct answer, overthinkers tend to default to thinking that there is one perfect solution. If they don't pick the correct item from the tome of a Cheesecake Factory menu, they will waste money and bring down the whole mood of their group. They will freeze and go back and forth, getting increasingly anxious about their choices since they put a lot of brain power into something inconsequential.

The need for perfectionism can also trigger a mind to go into hyperdrive. This goes back to all or nothing thinking discussed earlier, except in every facet of a person's life. Students who cried at a B+ grade may now revamp their study technique and punish themselves over a grade that others consider good. This person also quits a hobby because they are not an expert immediately. Despite having lives that we envy, they live on a tightrope.

The discomfort of any perceived failure feels like a blow torch on the palm of their hand. Their impatience, ego, and inability to apply criticism will doom them to a life of quiet quitting instead of going through the growing pains all the masters went through in their craft.

Finally, we have vulnerability. While vulnerability can be an external factor, there are times when it can be internal. People that are resistant to self-reflection fall into this trap. To grow, you must confront your flaws and be open to changing them. You may have to expose yourself to specific triggers and be alone with your thoughts. Meditating on your shortcomings is humbling and can cause a person to question themselves psychologically. Many would instead not go through this work and stagnate.

The Consequences of Overthinking

We hate ourselves for being such a downer, but often we wear these distortions like armor. It is all just mental clutter, taking valuable brainpower away from coping techniques and solutions. These effects can be both physical and mental.

The pathological response to stress is well documented (Bhandari, 2021). Your mind going a mile a minute all day is not a natural way to live. We all know the fight or flight response from acute stress, but the bigger enemy might be cortisol released during chronic stress. You might not be hyperventilating or ready to fight a tiger, but your body can never quite relax and is gearing something more akin to a period of starvation. Some effects include:

- increased heart rate
- pain from tense muscles and a digestive system in chaos

- overeating or malnutrition
- insomnia
- restlessness

The mental consequences can be even more complicated, feeding into feelings of inadequacy and despair. You may be unable to switch off these thoughts, but when you are folding laundry, your mind might start to race about upcoming bills. Or when you go to bed, the last thing you think about is how you feel your significant other will dump you any day now. Your mind is never quiet; worse, it tells you that you are worthless and deserve misfortune. You end up stuck in the past you would rather forget. Instead of focusing on good memories, you search for proof that the world is against you. Even if you learn a positive lesson, that black and white thinking will never allow you to grow and be confident. You will be stuck in student mode and feel you have nothing to offer someone else when it is invalid.

You can find yourself flip-flopping to extremes in how you navigate the world. You can fall into the trap of overplanning. These thoughts give you the illusion of thinking a problem through when really, you are just avoiding it. Plowing through these superficial thoughts and solving your issues will take much work and mental energy. It's like aiming a gun but never firing; what good is the bullet? You will be living your life on a hamster wheel, never making any progress. We get excited and plan or buy things when we start new things. It's a novel rush of dopamine that can be accomplished by hitting "add to cart", but it wears off quickly. This might explain the cemetery of abandoned hobbies overthinkers tend to have. You keep falling into this trap that starting a new program and buying this one really cool thing will finally be the thing that changes your life. If change were that easy, we wouldn't need therapists or books like these.

You might also avoid tasks that require your attention in order to put off the potential fallout. People with past financial problems may not open any of their bills or bank statements because they are afraid of what they might see. This Schrödinger's cat way of dealing with stress only delays the inevitable. The amount on your bill will not change just because you don't look at it. If anything, it will increase because of overdue fees.

Once you have burned out, you might find yourself in the f@&k it phase. This is when you are exhausted and stop caring about what you are doing. You start making compromises that would have shocked you from the beginning of the project. You start making silly mistakes and end up half-assing things in the end. Because you ran out of steam, you either ended up with another mess or something you hated.

Are you the type of person who can only seem to rise to the occasion when there is a fire under your butt? This is known as a "hot executive function". Either high rewards or serious consequences fuel these (Salehinejad et al., 2021). This is why you could cram a project into the night before. The entire time there was no urgency, just the nagging thought that the deadline was approaching. When it's the night before and you realize you will look like a fool if you don't start working, suddenly that fire is sparked, and you put your nose to the grindstone. You stress, swear, and gamble that you have everything you need while regretting not starting earlier. You vow you will never put yourself in that position again, but who are you kidding?

Hot executive function is not a bad thing. Being able to put your emotions in check during an emergency is extraordinary. If you are an overthinker and have never experienced a crisis, you have so many thoughts going on in your head at once that you freeze. Adults will forget basic information if they must relay it in a panic. Once you are seasoned, you can filter out all the noise and handle a situation that makes others panic. This takes a ton of practice and a willingness to get far out of your comfort zone. Still, that realization that at the moment of truth, time dilated, and everything you needed to do came to you clear as a bell, there is no better feeling.

"–Or everyone's gonna die." That is what they always say. But there's always a little bit of time before everybody dies– and that's when I do my best work.

–Peter B. Parker, Into the Spiderverse

What Can I Do?

Before we delve into the nitty-gritty of how to combat overthinking, you need to get yourself physically in a place that allows you to do so. That means getting proper sleep and knowing what focus feels like. These things take practice, dedication, and the ability to resist temptation.

The Most Overlooked Part of the Day: Bedtime

Sleep hygiene is essential to a restful night's sleep. It is the practice of creating an environment and a routine conducive to falling asleep and staying asleep. If you are tired, you will not have the energy to focus. We all have different habits, but in the age of social media and smartphones, that routine now includes scrolling in the dark until you fall asleep with your phone smacking you in the face. While this feels relaxing at the time, the light emitted from our phones tricks our brains into continuing to break down melatonin, like when the sun is up keeping us awake (*Blue Light Has a Dark Side*, 2012).

Creating a bedtime routine centered around winding down through self-indulgence is crucial. Many phones come with blue light filters that trigger on a timer you set. Still, you should wind down from stimuli about an hour before bedtime. Dim the lights, put away the phone, and settle in. Depending on your sensitivity and routine, showering in the morning is more helpful, as a night shower, with its noise and heat invigorate your senses instead of relaxing them.

Your bed is an essential part of the equation. If you eat or do work in your bed, stop. Your bed needs to be an escape; you should only associate it with relaxation, not spreadsheets and crumbs. Once you crawl into bed, you can read a book (not on your phone), meditate, journal, or focus on your senses. If your mind is still racing, put on some white noise to distract yourself from the day's worries. There are plenty of resources and devices for white noise. It doesn't need to be static; it can be rain, nature noises, quiet train noises, or any other calming environment you can think of. There are even podcasters that make content purposely boring yet calming enough to fall asleep to. Your bedtime routine should be your sanctuary; treat it as a form of self-care.

Mastering the Art of Focus

If you have been overthinking since childhood; you may have embedded being a scatterbrain into your identity. The idea that you can focus on anything that is not a screen seems laughable. Thanks to *Trataka Candle Gazing,* you can practice and get used to concentrating in a stress-free environment. While it is derived from meditation and hatha yoga, which has a spiritual aspect, it can be done by anyone. All you need is a candle (or any other accessible object to focus on) and a quiet, dimly lit room. Focus on the candle; if you feel yourself starting to pull away, bring your attention back to the light. The world should slowly fall away. Challenge yourself to one minute, then two, then five, and so on. You will accustom yourself to entering a flow state. Concentration is like a muscle; it takes work to flex it and can leave you exhausted if you are not used to it. By building your stamina, you are training yourself to work on more significant tasks for extended periods (Wilson, 2018).

Key Takeaways

- Our overthinking is a part of us that we have come to rely on. While there are benefits to a fast mind, it tends to be co-opted by our insecurities and fears.

- Overthinking can come from a few places such as past negative experiences, trauma, and being neurodivergent.

- Our brain is so loud in an effort to protect us that we live in a cage of our own making.

- You can understand your ruminations by familiarizing yourself with the different cognitive distortions that serve to warp your world.

- One of the first steps to mastering your more extreme emotions is to recognize your triggers. By seeing your thoughts and behavior as a response to an event, rather than in a vacuum, you can avoid scary situations and one day face them head on.

- If you don't fight rumination, the physical, mental, and social consequences can be potentially devastating.

- To begin this journey of decluttering your mind, you need to physically and mentally prepare. Getting a good night's sleep and practicing focus can help set the stage for progress.

FIRST STEPS TO
DECLUTTERING YOUR MIND

"If all I do is try, that means I don't truly believe I can succeed."

- KANAN JARUS, STAR WARS REBELS

Managing Stress in the Moment

Getting a handle on acute stress is critical to outgrowing an overactive fight or flight mindset. Stress breeds internal conflict that is noisy and unproductive. Your mind attempts to decipher a lot of information at once, and that surface layer analysis is biased by fear and insecurity. We have already accomplished the first step; we can give these thoughts names and uncouple them from our minds. Now the monster is at least outside the house, but it's still a problem since it's hissing, growling, and keeping us from the actual task at hand. But this monster has weaknesses that can be exploited.

Let's say you have been told to give your first technical talk in front of your peers at work. If you are an overthinker, your thoughts might be as follows:

- *They are all going to figure out I'm an idiot.*
- *They are going to notice I stutter a lot.*
- *I'm going to make the whole team look bad when I mess this up.*
- *They are never going to trust me with anything again.*

These thoughts are getting louder and more repetitive, and you might reach a bubbling over point if you don't act fast.

Don't Panic

A panic attack can compound a stressful event into a public and demoralizing spectacle. Anyone who has ever had panic attacks will tell you that becoming aware of an oncoming attack is like throwing kerosene on a fire (National Institute for Mental Health, n.d.). Signs include:

- pounding heart and tightening in the chest
- sweating
- nausea
- numbness in the extremities
- trouble breathing (hyperventilating)
- dizziness
- dry mouth

THE FIRST STEPS TO DECLUTTERING YOUR MIND

Okay, you can sense a panic attack coming. To stop yourself from falling, the best thing you can do is to focus on your senses. It resets your brain in a panic and lets it know that the room isn't on fire and has no reason to flip out. You can extend this exercise through the "54321 technique" ("The 54321 Grounding Technique For Anxiety," 2020).

- Look at five separate things and take in all the details, whether it's a nutrition label, the lines on your palm, or the petals on a flower.
- Touch or feel four objects within reach: how your clothes feel against your skin, the texture of your hair, or a warm mug.
- Listen for three things. They can be hum of the air conditioner, your breathing, or ambient chit-chat.
- Look out for two things you can smell, such as disinfectant or the lingering smell of detergent on your clothes.
- Taste one thing and note its flavor, temperature, and texture in your mouth.

Your symptoms should subside, but the source of your anxiety is still there. If you don't have a plan, you may spiral again.

Debating the Devil on Your Shoulder

Writing is a handy and therapeutic tool for this sort of introspection. We now have a label for these thoughts—cognitive distortions which we have already established are not rooted in logic. If you stop and think about them, your thoughts can probably be sorted into the cognitive distortion list in the previous chapter. You might even have a favorite. As terrifying as it sounds, these thoughts need to leave your head and become real either by speaking them out loud to someone else or (more conveniently) writing them down. Therapists assign homework like this in cognitive behavioral sessions. Let's try an example.

Q. What is the situation that is making you start to panic?

A. I have to give a talk at work.

Q. What thoughts are running through your head?

A. I will trip over my words, or someone will have questions I don't have an answer to. I am going to look like an idiot.

Q. What is the worst-case scenario if your fears are justified in this situation?

A. Everyone will laugh at me; no one will trust me with anything; all my hard work will be for nothing; I won't even trust myself anymore.

Q. How likely is this likely to happen? What evidence do you have?

THE FIRST STEPS TO DECLUTTERING YOUR MIND

> *A. Of course, I am a terrible speaker, but my boss has been friendly. I have worked on the project and have answered everyone's questions in private, and I have never seen anyone laughed out of the office, even when they did screw up. Now that I think about it, people have messed up before and it was never a big deal–maybe it's not as bad as I think it is.*

Q. What will most likely happen if your fears are justified?

> *A. If I mess up, then no one will care. I never have. My boss might give me pointers but won't yell at me. I just need to try again.*

Q. What are the chances you will be okay if the most likely outcome of your fear comes to fruition in a week? What about a month?

> *A. My pride might be bruised, but I will forget it in a week.*

Once you put pen to paper, you will realize that your worst fears sound silly. Cognitive distortions tend to collapse under even the slightest bit of scrutiny. You are not ignoring your distortions; you are interrogating them, asking them to justify taking up space in your brain.

Another technique you can try is imagining yourself advising someone else. Examine how you view the problem and talk about yourself objectively. Odds are you would probably give them sound advice and encourage them because, from an outsider's perspective, the problem has a solution. You would also be horrified if someone else talked about your friend the same way you talked about yourself. Treating ourselves with the same level of kindness we offer others should be aspired to. However, we often find it easier to be our worst critic because hearing it from ourselves is easier than from people we care about.

We need to stop breathing life into our self-doubt. We all have been or know someone who always calls attention to their perceived flaws. Self-effacing humor is fine in small doses, but there is a point where it starts to point to something more serious. We have all been or known someone who always calls attention to their perceived flaws.

- *Bear with me; I barely understand any of this.*
- *Ugh, I have a pimple, and it's bothering me.*
- *I am ugly.*
- *I am fat.*
- *Why do you even hang out with me?*
- *I'm probably not making any sense.*
- *Sorry if you have trouble understanding that my English is bad.*
- *Don't judge me, my house is a mess!* (There is one dish in the sink)

We do this because, once again, we are trying to control people's expectations and reactions to us. It may seem counterintuitive, but we would rather have a hand in our failure rather than disappoint someone in an earnest attempt to impress them. There is also the matter that our validation is not enough. Ironically, overthinkers who do poorly in social settings tend to care little about their own opinions. It does not matter if they feel like a model in their outfit; if one of their peers disagrees, they will crumble. We need validation from others, or our lives are meaningless.

Think Positive

Eliminating "should" statements in your internal monologue will change how you engage in your daily life. It's not just about banishing all bad thoughts, but about replacing them with good ideas that will motivate you throughout the day. The word "should" carries a deceptive amount of weight. It takes an action that would benefit us and puts a moralistic slant on it. This creates more black and white thought patterns that can demotivate us on a bad day. Not only that, have you ever refused to do something you were going to do because someone else told you to do it? We are perfectly capable of doing that to ourselves. *"I should get out of bed"* is often not enough motivation, but *"I would like to get out of bed so I can get ready in peace"* might be. You are introducing a positive outcome to your thought, even if it's just the idea that you are doing something you *want* instead of something you are obligated to do (Star, n.d).

Add more objectivity to your perceptions. When you become overwhelmed, even the simplest tasks, like brushing your teeth, can feel like a hassle. Your bed or phone is so enticing that you skip your nighttime routine, showering, brushing, and skin care. If you have found yourself underestimating how long you have spent on something enjoyable while overestimating how long something more mundane might take, you might be experiencing "time blindness". Later we will talk about how you can combat this all together, but with tasks that you constantly neglect, there is a hack you can try. If you have to wash the dishes but are tempted to skip them, try thinking, *"it will take ten minutes to wash the dishes."* Suddenly, cleaning up doesn't seem like a huge proposition. You can combine this with the "one-minute rule for cleaning". We have all heard this, if it takes you less than a minute to clean, just do it. You have to put the amount of time into your head, or you might ignore the task and cause it to snowball. Instead of just thinking to yourself, *"pick up those socks",* add the caveat, *"it will take you ten seconds to pick up those socks."*

The Science of Positive Thinking

Becoming your hype person is not just egotistical bunk, but a scientifically backed way to hack your brain into a more positive mindset. The brain has networks dedicated to self-processing (motivations and self-insight) and valuation. The valuation network is key because this region also focuses on rewards. While we usually associate rewards in science with a sweet treat for a mouse, the valuation system can also conceptualize abstract rewards in humans. Things like a sense of pride or a delayed reward are not the most tantalizing rewards, but as humans, to accomplish anything beyond eating and having sex, we have to have abstract motivations.

When scientists analyzed the brains of volunteers who were given a task, the group with positive affirmations had more activation of both brain regions than the group without affirmations. Positive affirmations also have a demonstrable effect on motivating people to go from being sedentary to performing physical tasks (Cascio et al., 2016).

So, how do you start? After all, there are affirmations everywhere, from whole books dedicated to them to wine mom t-shirts. Your affirmations should follow a few rules:

- They should be set in the present or future.
- They should be realistic; these are affirmations, not miracles.
- They should be tailored to you.
- You should be able to remember them if you are on the go easily.

Feel free to write your affirmations or speak them aloud over and over. (*Do Affirmations Work?*, 2020). Believe it or not, confidence requires practice. If you want to inspire yourself to work out, try:

- *I can become stronger.*
- *I can lift [insert weight here].*
- *I will practice until my form for [insert exercise] is perfect.*
- *Each time I go to the gym, it gets easier.*

Sitting and writing down affirmations may feel silly, but a custom statement will be more effective than canned affirmations. Next time you face a daunting undertaking, try having some affirmations under your belt and stick them on a post-it for quick motivation.

Key Takeaways

- Learning to center yourself in a moment of crisis can help you manage your acute stress and avoid panic.
- Becoming aware of your senses is your best tool to ground yourself.
- Break your need to manage the emotions of others by pointing out negativity.
- Sometimes it is necessary to debate our baser instincts: write your thoughts and emotions down. You should be able to look at the facts in an objective manner.
- Chores that can seem daunting or annoying lose their power when you remind yourself that most of them take mere minutes to complete.
- Positive affirmations can hack your brain into having a better outlook.

FORGIVING PAST YOU
SO PRESENT YOU CAN INVEST IN FUTURE YOU

"One problem with gazing too frequently into the past is that we may turn around to find the future has run out on us."

- MICHAEL CIBENKO

James has been working hard on himself, and tonight he will enjoy the fruits of his labor. He has a date. After months of getting out of his comfort zone and getting used to talking to others, he finally had the courage to ask a girl out and she said yes. This should be a happy moment, but James has been a wreck all day. He cannot help but dwell on how poorly his last relationship went.

Three years ago, he began a relationship with a woman named Shannon. She was smitten, and things were going well for about a year. However, James started to change. He began getting colder, work had been putting a ton of pressure on him, and he could not muster the same emotional connection he once had. He could not explain it, but he started to put distance between himself and Shannon.

To try and rectify things, Shannon bent over backward to get James to care for her again. She made his meals, listened to his frustrations, and put a lot of effort into the bedroom, thinking it was her fault that things had changed. In reality, nothing she did or could do could change James. Before he knew it, the relationship had broken Shannon, and she left. James was dumbfounded, and as he talked to people about it, he realized how his behavior had hurt the person he cared for the most. When he contacted Shannon, she confirmed everything and clarified that she was ready to move on. James understood; he didn't do it on purpose but did not notice how much suffering he had caused under his nose, which disgusted him.

James sought therapy and took some time off the dating scene. Through his sessions, he realized that his coldness might have resulted from self-sabotage and insecurity. Learning his ego was the cause of his current misery, James vowed to become more conscientious, but it quickly became overthinking. Subconsciously, he did not feel he deserved Shannon, and she would eventually figure it out and leave him. He decided to beat her to the punch and disconnect.

As he was getting ready for his date, he realized he wanted it to go well; therefore, he had something to lose. Looking back at his messages, he judged them for being too closed off, not funny, or too desperate. It didn't matter that his date continued to show interest; she was wrong. She wouldn't last more than an hour talking to him. Either she would see right through him—a jerk with no redeeming qualities—or she would fall for him, and he would only hurt her.

James recognized himself spiraling and realized he needed to get a hold of himself. He is not the person he was two years ago. His date checked in within the hour, meaning she would probably not flake and is interested. This should be a fun night; spending it stewing on his past will ruin it. He repeated to himself:

- *I would like to have a good time tonight.*
- *I have grown up a lot since my last relationship.*
- *I have to give her and myself a chance.*
- *I will not sabotage something good because I am afraid.*

With his head screwed on a bit straighter, James went on his date and had a good time.

Growth is complicated and frustrating, and the easiest person to take all our pent-up rage out on is the past version of ourselves. That person and the choices they made seem alien to you. Unfortunately, anger at and fear of that person can hinder your journey. You need to forgive that person for mastering yourself.

Don't Let Comparison Steal Your Joy

Slave to the Timeline

Time is the resource we fear taking for granted. We are conditioned from birth to adhere to strict developmental and social timelines. We must walk, talk, read, write, and use the bathroom at a critical time or risk bringing shame onto our parents and our toddler selves. Our education track tends to solidify in late elementary and middle school, with honors programs, musical instruments, and extracurriculars being introduced around this time. Being put in the "slower" class can set you behind for the rest of your academic career. Likewise, once a child is placed in the honors track, they tend to stay there as the classes are smaller, the teachers more attentive, and every adult tells them how great they are.

For a child to break into that track, they need to be exceptional and fight the inherent negative bias they have had since kindergarten. It might not be that this child is less capable than the honors kids, they might have an unstable home life with no access to tutors or coaches, or they might have dealt with a challenging year that had their education take a back seat. While coping with academic pressures, students are expected to have a ton of friends, attend clubs, and do sports. They are exposed to media where the entire school revolves around friends engaging in hijinks and wacky fun. This overly idealized version of life is normalized on top of the pressure of doing well in school. Adults they trust tell kids that if they don't do well and go to college, that they will be doomed to a life as a loser. The result is a generation of burned-out kids that grow into anxious or cynical adults.

By our mid-twenties, we must have our own place, a car, and a vibrant social life. Romantically, if you are a man, you need to lose your virginity as early as possible and woo a woman easily. If you are a woman, you need to be in a relationship, and if you don't have children by the age of 30, you might as well get a bunch of cats and call it a day. Romantic expectations are so ingrained in young adults that they tie their entire self-worth around the ability to attract a partner. Are they rich enough, are they pretty enough, are they enough? Loneliness and rejection is now an epidemic in modern adults and many simply cannot cope.

There are many legitimate reasons why your timeline might not look the same as those of your peers. Mental health, economic hardship, health issues, life's unpredictability, and the simple fact that we are all different can throw a timeline out of whack. Despite this, we often feel shame for not accomplishing as much as our peers, especially during our youth. There is an adage that "youth is wasted on the young" that boomers like to tout to deal with their regrets. This is also permeated by hustle culture that will tell you that everyone who does not wake up at 5 a.m. to work their three jobs to afford a luxury apartment is just not trying hard enough. This narrow view of success leads people to do impulsive things like pursuing a degree they don't care about or starting a family with the wrong person just because they feel they should.

Age is a powerful bias. Youth is power, and society labels you as disposable once you age out of being able to date Leonardo DiCaprio. People hear that they should enjoy the years when they have no kids and no back pain, while at the same time they need to focus on the future and meet all the arbitrary benchmarks. In this economy, the balance is nearly impossible for the average person. The race to be rich, beautiful, and married can be untenable.

If we subscribe to the importance of timelines, we set arbitrary limits on ourselves. Aging is a gift many are not afforded and should be the subject of gatekeeping. Don't be afraid to start being active or creative as an adult. It can be disheartening to compare yourself with someone who started a similar pursuit as a child or be in a university surrounded by people 15 years younger than you. But you have a choice. You can begin college and get a degree when you are 40, or you can be 40 with no degree. Aging is inevitable, but continued growth is not. Do not let age be an excuse to stagnate.

Finding the Right Inspiration

Finding that jolt of inspiration can help you start the hard stuff. However, content that floats to the top of web searches tends to be about getting us to consume rather than improve ourselves. There are some great content creators out there with a wealth of knowledge and exhilarating stories of self-discovery, but this is like finding a needle in a haystack. Inspiring content can be performative for the sake of the mighty algorithm and is infeasible for the average person to maintain. This is not helped by the hustle culture that emphasizes quick and easy returns, which we have established as a fantasy time and time again. As consumers of media, we love an inspiring story with linear progress. Prep and failure do not make for sexy content. Think of these journeys as great photos. We are only interested in the final product and not the hours of setup, hundreds of shots, and heavy post-production that go into creating a once-in-a-lifetime image.

Anyone can claim to be an expert on anything if they know how to package their information in a way that sounds credible. Online dieting and fitness content is probably the worst offender of this. A 20 year old with no college degrees or certifications can peddle misinformation with such confidence and charm that they sound credible. Some of these gurus have achieved incredible results, but there are other factors at play such as youth, an easier lifestyle, and having the money to afford an expensive gym membership, diet plan, and health insurance. You need to be able to cut through the riffraff for any research and inspiration you are seeking. The only foolproof method is to remain skeptical and use various resources. Remember:

It is important to draw wisdom from different places. If you take it from only one place, it becomes rigid and stale.

- Uncle Iroh, Avatar the Last Airbender

Cross-reference, seek out reviews, and most importantly, if a particular piece of advice is not working for you, do not try and force it. Not every book or podcast will apply to your life. Remaining flexible with your expectations will help manage your emotions. Not allowing yourself to break down in the face of disappointment will give you the capacity to pivot.

Forgive Yourself

Luke Skywalker: I don't believe it.

Yoda: That is why you fail.

- Star Wars: The Empire Strikes Back

To move forward, the next step is to forgive the past version of you. They did their best with what they had and what they knew. Hindsight bias is a powerful thing, and it can make the past version of you look stupid in comparison to present you. Real self-improvement never comes from a place of self-loathing, even if you don't identify with the person that you were. It comes from loving yourself enough to do better.

No More Negative Self-Talk

There is a difference between being aware of your flaws and self-flagellating to the point of suffering. One is born of emotional intelligence and a need to improve, the other comes from self-hatred and a need to take your frustrations out on something–even if it's yourself. Do you ever find yourself thinking to yourself:

- *I am stupid.*
- *I am a failure.*
- *What is wrong with me?*
- *I deserve this.*
- *Why did I think I could do this?*
- *Why does anyone listen to me?*

These thoughts are not productive, and they personalize every issue in your life, warping them into character flaws. If you could not do mental math in front of someone else, it's not that you were having an off day, it's that you are intrinsically bad at math or worse–that you are a moron.

You start to create an identity out of your weaknesses instead of your strengths and this can have a serious impact on your trajectory. You might avoid entire subjects, situations, and opportunities because you have this bias that you are wholly incapable. Get the notion of

"I can't" out of your head. Will you be a master at first? No, of course not, but you will be better than every person who never bothers trying.

Try this thought exercise. Let's say you are drawing something but are disheartened by your own progress. Most of your thoughts are probably in the flavor of:

- *I suck at drawing.*
- *Why am I wasting my time on this?*
- *This is so bad I should cut off my hands to never blight the world with something so ugly again.*

Now, reframe those thoughts as if your friend drew the picture. Would you say those things to them or point out how much better they are getting? More importantly, how would you respond if a stranger told your friend the same thing you tell yourself? You would probably fly into a rage–so why don't you have that same energy for yourself?

If you find the voice in your head acting more like a movie drill sergeant, you should attempt to reframe these thoughts. "I am stupid" can become "I am excited to learn about this"; instead of "I still can't squat my goal weight," try "this weight is getting easier." There is nothing naive about looking at your world through a glass-half-full perspective. Ultimately, you are still looking at the same glass, but how those thoughts mingle in your head is much healthier and can even improve your cognitive performance (Kim et al., 2021). If you don't believe that you are capable of succeeding, then you never will.

Another thing you can do is eliminate any variety of the polarizing "should" statement.

- I should get out of bed.
- I should go to the gym.
- I should sign up for that class.
- I should study more.

These statements not only create a binary set of outcomes where failure becomes an option, but it also introduces almost a moral stance on your decisions. Plus, there are many things we should do, and that vague notion is not great motivation. We tend to associate things we are supposed to do with unpleasant feelings. When we think about getting up for work, we might find ourselves dreading traffic or a boring meeting on the docket. Who wouldn't want to stay in their warm bed after that? Humans seek rewards, so play to that when you are trying to psych yourself up.

- *I am going to feel great after I work out.*
- *I would like to get out of bed so I can eat breakfast.*
- *If I head over to work, I can get myself that iced coffee I like on the way.*

- *I am as prepared for this test as I can be, I am proud of how hard I worked.*

Invoking positive feelings as opposed to feeling coerced by expectations will help the present you deal with anything that might come your way.

Looking Towards the Future

Now that you have been doing a ton of introspection and have been handling your overthinking at the moment, it's time to think about what the future holds. Your racing mind has probably been holding you back from the person you want to be. Remember, it's not a race, and so long as you commit to consistency and patience, you will become your ideal you. These goals might be a bit abstract and overwhelming, but there is a useful thought exercise you can try:

Think about being on your deathbed after you have lived a long life. What do you think your thoughts will be in those moments? According to nurses, regret–not chronic illness–tends to lead to the saddest last moments. Whether it was not spending more time with family, not pursuing a dream, or not having enough fun, these regrets crystallize when people are out of time (Steiner, n.d.). No one is advising you to bankrupt yourself or engage in dangerous behavior, but it is more likely that you will regret not investing in learning something new like cooking or archery than having a bit less money at the moment of your death.

Thanks to capitalism, most people will be remembered as cogs in a large machine, there to produce and make money for the powers that be. Not many people in this world will say they wish they spent more hours working (this is different from wishing you had more money). But in the present moment, it's the only way they know how to survive.

Something you should ponder is what your relationship to your own anxiety is. As unpleasant as it is, anxiety can act as a security blanket we carry because we are in survival mode. Anxiety and overthinking are so embedded in our personalities and habits, we might fear that we might be lesser than without it. There is savviness and there is rumination; one gives you a leg up in the world, and the other is a cinder block around your ankles. The first habit you need to break is thinking you need that negative voice in your head screaming at you (Brewer, 2021). For this, you may need to call in the big guns.

Calling For Help

Some people dig themselves into such a deep mental hole that they will need help climbing out. While a trusted family member or friend can be a good start, a licensed therapist and even medication can be legitimate solutions. Asking for professional help is nothing to be ashamed of, and medications are not a cheat. Self-improvement still takes time and work even with these tools. Still, the process can be mind-bogglingly difficult and diametrically opposed to an overthinker. Oftentimes you are at the mercy of a search engine and your insurance or budget to filter your choices. Mental health professionals come in all certifications and specialties. They may specialize in one age group, demographic, or disorder. For a chronic ruminator, bearing your soul in an email to a psychologist only to find out they specialize in pediatric autism will be too embarrassing to bear.

The initial therapy sessions can be intimidating. Part of the intake process is an interview where the therapist takes a full mental history. You have to open up to this stranger with a fancy degree on a couch while talking about every traumatizing moment of your life. While therapists should be professional and handle more sensitive topics with care, the patient might be uncomfortable and exhausted after these sessions. If the first therapist does not work out, you will most likely have to go through the intake process again, which can be too much to handle (Kleiven et al., 2020).

There are also different types of therapy and formats. Group therapy can be validating and is often cheaper than individual sessions. However, you may not be as inclined to be completely honest if you are in a room with 10 other people. Virtual sessions give people many more options since the distance is no longer a factor (though some state licenses limit practice to be solely within that state). The one caveat is that virtual sessions can feel less personal and even awkward (Flynn, 2020). Your first therapist may not even be the best fit. Luckily, you can switch providers any time you want. This is completely normal in the mental health world and a professional should be understanding of that fact. If they are not, then they are probably not a good provider anyway. Then there is the biggest sticking point, and that is methods. While there is a veritable collection of philosophies, the two most common ones are Cognitive Behavioral Therapy (CBT) and Acceptance and Commitment Therapy (ACT).

CBT is the style of therapy we have discussed the most thus far. At its core, it is the acknowledgment of our negative feelings and thought patterns as irrational and making a conscious effort to change that pattern. It goes back to the car alarm analogy: the problem is not the noise itself, it's the fact that a bird landing on the hood caused it. It is a highly effective form of therapy and is probably the technique people associate the most with therapy. Through talking out issues, recognizing distortions, and working towards rewiring our brains to stop self-destruction, anxiety, depression, alcoholism, OCD, and many other ailments have an avenue of non-chemical treatment.

People like the structure the sessions have as well as the introduction of self-control and empowerment. While you can't talk some external issues away, you can train yourself to deal with them in a more productive manner.

CBT is not for everyone though and that can lead to people thinking that therapy all together is useless. CBT requires a person to put in a lot of work. They have to be vulnerable, remember and attend their appointments, do the take-home assignments, and be in a place where they can be completely honest with their therapist. A person who is at rock bottom or who has difficulty trusting others may not be capable of this. CBT might not actually address your external world when it comes to treatment.

Having a therapist tell you your reaction to certain things is irrational can read as condescending, especially if that therapist is inexperienced. The onus is on the patient to improve their mindset, but some things in life are genuinely distressing and some of the advice reads as "buck up buttercup it's all in your head". Say you have a person who is afraid of dogs after they were bitten as a child. CBT would tell them that their adrenaline pumping and freezing at the sound of a bark should be trained out of them. That doesn't change the fact that this person was genuinely hurt by the animal and that to a degree, their fears are not unfounded. CBT will probably not be too effective on this person.

Luckily, there is more than one way to skin a cat. ACT is similar to CBT except that it involves *acceptance* of your feelings instead of *rejecting* them. Your fears are valid, but you practice separating them from yourself. Instead, you learn to observe yourself, warts and all, with kinder non-judgmental eyes and work towards matching your values. The patient who was bitten by a dog may work on becoming more comfortable with dogs if she wishes but will also be validated if she does not want to associate with them. It takes into account the unpredictability of this world and allows you to be human and imperfect. If you want to be rid of your symptoms, ACT is probably not for you. The emphasis is to learn to live with them. This form of therapy might be more accessible to someone who cannot put in the same amount of work and cognitive rewiring that CBT requires. Both methods are peer-reviewed and have a parade of success stories around them (*ACT vs. CBT*, 2022).

Key Takeaways

- You have to declutter your mind of pointless timelines. This can be difficult because we have been chained to them since childhood.

- Our mind is littered with comparing ourselves to total strangers while we wonder why we cannot succeed in the same way.

- If you want to go out and do something, your age should never get in the way. It's never too late to start something new.

- If you only do something out of an obligation to check off an item on society's idea of a good life, you may end up doing something you regret. Do things because you want to.

- Inspiration is great but be sure it is not giving you an unrealistic expectation.

- Forgive yourself for not having hindsight.

- No one has the right to insult you, that includes you!

- Eliminate "should" statements to motivate yourself.

- You may find yourself thinking about how you want your future to look. You are going to need to do a ton of introspection on what inner demons are holding you back.

- Therapy can be a fantastic way to get to the source of your ruminations.

OVERTHINKING AND OUR RELATIONSHIPS

"Maybe some people just aren't meant to be in our lives forever. Maybe some people are just passing through. It's like some people just come through our lives to bring us something: a gift, a blessing, a lesson we need to learn. And that's why they're here. You'll have that gift forever."

- DANIELLE STEELE, THE GIFT

Jacob has been debating going after an undergraduate degree in computer science. He is 35 with a wife and son and has decided he needs to take a risk to make a better life for his family. Jacob had worked as a waiter since he was a teenager, but the long hours, inconsistent pay, and resulting chronic back pain were all taking their toll. He worked out the logistics so that he could take online classes at a cheap college and keep working full-time. Jacob decided to ask around, and for the most part, everyone was supportive. His wife was excited about the prospect and his parents were proud and even offered to babysit if he needed it. Sadly, his friend group did not share the enthusiasm. When Jacob floated the idea, they laughed in his face recalling how much he hated math as a teenager, joked about his short attention span, and felt the whole thing was a waste of time and money.

Their reaction took Jacob aback. He thought that his childhood friends, of all people, should have believed in him. Jacob left that conversation with doubts. Maybe he just wasn't a "college guy". Maybe he should stick to waiting tables since he was good at it. It wasn't the most glamorous life, but there was comfort in sticking with what he knew.

The opinions of others, even strangers, can be catalysts for overthinking. It's one thing when we have our own quiet doubts, but when an outsider shares those feelings, it solidifies them. Positive feedback can be incredibly validating, while even mild criticism can destroy a person's confidence, even if the other party did not intend to do so.

The people we choose to surround ourselves with can make or break our journey. A person who is in recovery from alcoholism is often advised that they should be prepared to lose all their friends. The social aspect of drinking is enticing, and "bar friends" may minimize recovery or project their own insecurities onto a person who is trying to improve their own life. We aim to please the people we consider friends and tolerate a lot of abuse. If you choose to attempt to let the negative influence roll off your back, you risk that person becoming a second devil on your shoulder urging you to give in for old time's sake.

The people in our lives have just as much to do with our progress as we do. They can motivate us and give us a shoulder to cry on, or they can weigh us down. Changing is an inherent part of self-improvement and some people might see that change as unnecessary or even a betrayal. This is known as the "crabs in a bucket phenomenon". If you have ever been around people who hunt crabs you are probably already familiar with this. When you catch a crab and put it in a bucket, you do not need a lid. This is because the crabs will actually pull down their comrade who is close to making an escape.

Humans can behave the same way. A person who is seeking an education might be called an elitist for daring to think above their station. Famously, when Adele chose to lose weight due to her declining health, she was the subject of ridicule for "giving into beauty standards", "selling out", and betraying all the women in larger bodies who might have looked to her as inspiration.

People change, they grow apart, and they can hurt each other. Forgiveness or burning bridges can both be appropriate actions depending on the circumstances. Our own self-esteem is often predicated on what the people around us think. You might think you are making great progress, but even an offhand comment can completely derail you. Still, humans are social animals, and we derive our value from the number and quality of our relationships. Learning to combat overthinking in regard to our peers might be one of the harder things to learn.

Projecting Our Own Insecurities

As we have established, we tend to assume our thought process is similar to others. That's why when we are low, we tend to isolate ourselves or over-assume how critical a person is. Since we are not exactly jazzed with ourselves, we assume others feel the same. It's the classic mind reader cognitive distortion at play and it can destroy your relationships and become a self-fulfilling prophecy of loneliness.

To see an example of projection putting a relationship in jeopardy, one has to look no farther than the cinematic masterpiece of Shrek 2. The movie starts with a newlywed Shrek and Fiona enjoying their honeymoon. In the adorable frolicking montage, there is no indication that Fiona is dissatisfied with her new husband and being an ogre. She embraces her new freedom despite having to make a number of compromises (that she accepts with grace) in her new life. Shrek, on the other hand, starts to feel insecure, especially after meeting Fiona's family. There, he is confronted with the fact that Fiona was meant to marry a handsome prince rather than a swamp dwelling beast.

Tension only starts to emerge between the couple when Shrek and Fiona's father, the king, begin sniping at each other. Instead of talking to his wife and realizing that she was happy and would never turn her back on him, Shrek concocted a plan involving a fairy godmother (who turned out to be evil, but he didn't know that), a magic potion, and a midnight kiss to become the ideal handsome husband that he felt that Fiona deserved. Fiona was never going to leave and had to be put under a spell for the sake of the climax of the film where it looked like she and Shrek were done for. By the end of the movie, Fiona didn't change all that much. Shrek was the one with the character arc of becoming more secure in his relationship and trusting Fiona.

Have you ever felt awkward about reaching out to a friend or planning an event? There might be an inherent amount of social anxiety or a rotten memory at play. Someone might have disappointed you back in the day and it was easier to personalize this event than admit that our friend may not have our back. What thoughts go through your head when it comes to trying to socialize?

- *They are going to think it's weird if I reach out.*
- *They have more important things to do than hang out with me.*
- *What would we even do? I don't want to bore them.*

Loneliness is painful but it's at least familiar, and even comfortable. We only have our own expectations to manage and ourselves to disappoint. We put our friends and family on this pedestal, so they don't muddy their shoes with our issues. This might work for some people, but for others, there will be that painful realization that you have no one to share your brightest moments with. This can be worse than any other social faux pas we might commit, but there is a way to dig out of it.

A friendship is not an artifact in a museum to be stared at from a distance and never handled. It needs to come out of the glass case and be played with or else it fades away. Think of someone you get along with but haven't seen in a while, or a friend that is always initiating plans. How would you react if they asked you to go out to lunch or for a drink? You would probably be over the moon.

So why do you think that their reaction to you asking to hang out would be any different? Remember our cognitive distortion exercises. Their most likely reaction would probably be "of course I want to see you, it's been too long!" They might also feel relieved as they too might have thought it was a bit awkward reaching out after so long. The worst outcome is that they can't hang out, but even then, they probably aren't going to laugh behind your back about it. Either way, you have an answer you can act on. You are free to tend to the relationship and make it stronger or find greener pastures.

Understanding Overthinking Others

Whether it's just an overabundance of caution or diagnosable social anxiety, the opinions of others can be kryptonite. Relationships at every level, from acquaintance to significant other, can suffer once rumination takes hold. We tend to project our own opinions and values onto others to understand them. It can feel like our only tool because of a fear of communication or confrontation. We think we are mind readers.

However, all we are doing is subjecting others to unfair preconceived notions. We think of ourselves as the main character because sonder (the fact that every person on the planet has lived a life as complicated as yours) is too much to grasp. This communication breakdown can lead to distance and a subtle phasing out of a relationship. You know, the type when you realize that you have not talked to someone you could not imagine your life without at one point in several months, and neither of you has seemed to notice.

If you were around in the 1980s and 1990s, your trips to the supermarket included lines of tabloids documenting the downfall of the marriage between Princess Diana and Prince Charles of Wales. If you are younger or have never seen *The Crown*, Prince Charles was first in line for the throne and was matched with Lady Diana Spencer for her good looks, pedigree, and innocent appearance. She was meant to follow tedious royal protocol, make a few media appearances, and pump out a few heirs. Instead, Diana became a sensation, universally loved by people worldwide for her grace, humility, and connection to the common person.

As the future king, Charles was supposed to be the star of every engagement, but Diana quickly overshadowed him. Charles was stuffy, boring, and a symbol of old royalty and could not measure up to the charm his wife had on everyone they met and, most importantly, the media. To Charles, this was a disaster. Diana had to avoid heels not to be taller than her husband, dress modestly, and deal with Charles's very public affair. With no outlet for her despair, Diana's mental health also crumbled. She developed an eating disorder and even attempted to end her life by throwing herself down the stairs. All because she shone brighter than the crown.

To the royal family, Diana was young, naive, an outsider, and a bit of a rebel; she should never have been the face of the crown, but she started to eclipse even Elizabeth. The relationship had started on a high note, but thanks to resentment and wandering eyes on both sides, it ended in divorce. Since the crown is also the head of the church of England, the future king being unable to honor the sanctity of his marriage was, to say the least, not a good look. However, the relationship had become so toxic that they had no other recourse in the end. The crown would have been lucky to have such a popular face. The days of unconditional reverence for the royal family were over. The people were disillusioned, and the tabloids were relentless. Since no one in the Windsor family could see beyond their ego, they crushed Diana instead of letting her do some much-needed rehab on their image (Nast, 2022).

The waters in relationships can also become murky because of the added vulnerability that comes with it. No one wants to be made a fool of. Betrayal hurts on an emotional level and can challenge your notion of masculinity and femininity. Self-worth often rides on a successful courtship.

As a result, when someone starts to act even slightly off, people assume the worst. If you look at relationship advice boards, you would think that a person becoming a little more emotionally cold doesn't love you any more or that a person having any sort of friend of the opposite gender means they are cheating. Instead of simply asking the questions, people will self-sabotage by creating distance, projecting their insecurities, and starting pointless arguments. Arguing, in general, is also common in people with ADHD. This disorder is not just about the inability to focus; it also comes with memory issues, mood dysregulations, sensory issues, and the tendency to raise your voice, which can cause full-blown arguments (Kubala, 2022).

Regardless of why a relationship may end, you will be left with feelings of loneliness and inadequacy. You might be able to start again with new friendships or you might go down one of two paths: isolation or people-pleasing.

Handling the End of The Line

The end of a friendship or a romantic relationship can be a devastating experience if you have no choice in the matter. Rejection can make us feel naked, as though our flaws have caught up to us and were exposed to a person we value. Relationships can end with a boom, or they can fade away quietly. Regardless, it is a painful experience that needs to be dealt with. If not, you will be doomed to overthink all your relationships going forward.

Even though no one has died, grief is a perfectly valid response to a breakup, even if it is a platonic relationship (Segal, 2023). Your life has changed, and a source of validation, comfort, and security has vanished. Your thoughts will twist and turn as you ruminate every interaction and possibility. Coming to terms with these emotions—not burying them—is the only way to stop your head from spinning.

It might seem easier to pretend you aren't bothered by the rejection, but it is a natural human emotion that needs processing. Cry, journal, rant to a trusted friend or therapist—anything to organize your thoughts. You might realize that there were things you could have done better or that the relationship was toxic all along. This experience might end up being a net positive in the end.

Lessons From Rejection

We aren't perfect, so mistakes can happen even if you genuinely care about another person. While you shouldn't dissect every moment of your time together, you should delve deep and examine the big things you might have missed. This will only work if you break free from disorganized overthinking and parse things out one at a time with kind eyes. If your inner voice is too harsh, you might feel defensive. Some questions you can ask to keep focused include:

- Did I take this relationship for granted?
- Did I communicate my feelings or assume the other person understood me?
- Did I start to get cold?
- Did the other person start to get distant?
- Did my significant other spell out what they needed, and did I not take it to heart?
- Why were we compatible in the first place, and did that change?
- Are there any red flags I missed?

You can examine all this and work on yourself. A common phenomenon is sabotaging a relationship due to insecurity either in oneself or in the relationship. Sometimes this can result in arguments or becoming emotionally distant. Either the person thinks they can do better or think their partner is too good for them and will leave at the first opportunity. The result is the same: subconsciously, they start to check out of the relationship. That "comes to Jesus' moment", where you realize how your actions may have hurt another person—even if you didn't realize it—may be the catalyst for a newer, brighter relationship.

Some relationships are better off in the past either because of the malice of one party or overall incompatibility. These are the relationships your overthinking brain may try to justify staying in rather than retreating. Breaking things off solidifies that you were played, were not as good a judge of character as you thought you were and lost your precious time. This is the sunk cost fallacy at work; if you are not careful, you will spend more time and energy on something that ultimately harms you.

Humans can be downright irrational in the name of acceptance. The *Asch Conformity Experiments* highlighted this sociological quirk where people would reject an obviously right answer if the entire room disagrees (Mcleod, 2022). When we are outnumbered, our brain does some serious gymnastics to conform. We gaslight ourselves into thinking we are crazy. So, the answer to your mother's question, "if all your friends drove off a cliff, would you go as well?" is a resounding *yes*. It doesn't even have to be a crowd. A single person can turn the tide of your brain. You have a physiological response to giving in to pressure; your reward centers light up more than if you decided for yourself (Bault et al., 2011). This evolutionary trait might have come in handy when we were in caves and were pressured not to eat a poison bush, but today it just gets us in trouble.

A person is smart. People are dumb, panicky, dangerous animals and you know it.

- Agent K, Men in Black

Maybe getting out of that swirl of influence is the best thing. You can find out who you are without the pressure of acceptance. Only then can you figure out what you want in life, where your values are, and what kind of people you want to surround yourself with.

Cutting People Out

For your sake, the only way to maintain your sanity is to cut people out. You have to look out for yourself, and if you have an emotional vampire in your life, you have to drive a stake into their metaphorical heart. Sometimes a person might not even be a malicious person; you can just be completely wrong for each other. Unless this person is a literal child who depends on you, no one is entitled to your energy, and you are allowed to protect yourself.

A relationship is a lot like the super soldier serum in Marvel Comics. When someone takes it, their good traits become great; the bad get worse. Tenderness, vulnerability, and unconditional love can reveal a wondrous side of you that you never knew you had. However, these traits can make someone complacent, make them give into their baser instincts, and bring out the worst version of themselves.

Then there is the relationship where one party is trying to improve, while the other becomes resentful of the change. You might be dubbed a sell-out or trying to reach above your station for having the audacity to improve. Let's go back to the alcoholic's example. There are a few reasons these relationships are doomed, and it's rarely because the sober party has done something wrong:

- The bar is central to the relationship, and the friends may not be willing to change that.

- Supporting an addict requires support from the village. That means no more drinking in front of this person, offering emotional stability, and holding the sober person accountable. In short, some may see it as too much work.

- The addict and the sober person were once on even footing, meaning that change is possible. It is much harder being complacent in unhealthy behaviors when your friend is no longer backing you up. Peer pressure can be positive, albeit uncomfortable. This can lead to defensiveness and even sabotage.

You are already in a precarious situation, wondering if the change is worth it and battling the worst version of yourself. There are also physical withdrawal symptoms that can tempt you back to ease the pain. Now you may have someone who is real, whose opinion matters to you feeding into those emotions. Cutting a person out might just be your only option if they seem dead set on sticking to their habits. Remember your values and what your grand vision for your life is while you decide your course of action. By using these instead of ruminating, a decision will become clear.

Time to be the Bad Guy

When cutting a person out, you become the bad guy in their story. People pleasers and those with a positive bias towards your former friend will be pushing for your forgiveness. You might have tried to push this person away before, but this time the offender swears they can change, things will be different. They may cry, beg, and in extreme cases threaten to harm themselves if you are no longer in their lives. Guilt and a false sense of responsibility will start to cloud your judgment. This person could have physically harmed us or financially ruined someone, but there still exists that tiny part in their brain that wants to go back to the good times. Personalization starts to creep in, and you will think to yourself: *If I am better, they will go back to the way they were before!*

If they were capable of changing, they would do so, regardless of whether they are in your life or not. Sometimes rejection is a necessary consequence that might catalyze change. This toxic person can have two choices:

- They can do some self-reflection and realize how problematic their behavior has been. They should resolve to change for the sake of being a better person—not as a means to an end.
- They can also double down on their behavior and blame the other person for abandoning them.

You do not need to be there to find out.

Signs You Should Look for The Escape Hatch

Sometimes it can be challenging to ascertain if a relationship is going through normal ebbs and flows or is unsalvageable. Your mind is screaming about social pressures to see the best in others, not to be selfish, and to remember all the good times.

Friendship and romance are supposed to be fun; when you start feeling like you need to walk on eggshells and happy when you know you don't have to see them, it might be time to look for the escape hatch. A person shows their true colors when they encounter a person that is of no benefit to them.

- Have they blamed you for their troubles?
- Have they tried to guilt you with phrases such as:
    - Don't you care about me?
    - I guess I'll just be miserable without you!
    - This stress is going to cause (insert consequence here).
    - You aren't even giving me a chance (you have given them multiple chances).
    - How could you do this to me?
    - Well, I guess I'm just the worst (insert relation here) aren't I?
- Have they tried to deflect blame onto you when you explain their behavior?
- Have they given a proper apology? Red flags for a bad apology include:
    - I am sorry you were offended!
    - It's my fault for trusting you!
    - I was only messing with you!
    - Sorry! Can we move on?

This person's brain is working overtime to avoid an ego hit. Most of these phrases deal with their emotions or how your emotions were a burden. A toxic person will never admit that their actions were wrong or that your emotions are validated. These are signs this person has not learned anything and is more concerned with preserving the status quo. You should not put an ounce of thinking into debating whether this person is worthy of your time.

Forgiving Others

Thanks to religion (mainly Judeo-Christian), our culture is obsessed with forgiveness. When a person is biased towards the perpetrator or was not involved in the dispute, they tend to pressure you towards absolving. Even though it was never their apology to accept, you will hear the cavalcade of "they said they were sorry, what more do you want?" or "you know it's bad to hold a grudge", or the ever popular "you are being petty". In reality, most of these are based on the desire for things to return to normal. Having people in your life fight is naturally uncomfortable, and it would be simpler if both parties kissed and made up as opposed to having to pick a side or, *gasp*, holding someone accountable. Regardless, if a person has hurt you, then it is not on you to ensure the continuation of the group dynamic, especially at the cost of your peace.

If you are going to forgive, it doesn't have to be for the sake of the other person's feelings. It can be for your own well-being. Grudges are toxic and holding on to those negative feelings can impact your ability to live your life going forward. You may be projecting those negative emotions on everything that so much as reminds you of the past. Part of forgiveness is coming to terms with the hurt and vulnerability that you felt. You are essentially acknowledging that someone else had that much power over you. You have to allow yourself to feel those emotions, so they stop buzzing endlessly in your head. You don't have to allow this person back into your life. They don't even have to know you took on this journey of forgiveness. You just need to release those feelings after fully processing them. If you see that this person has made a real change without your input and has made a genuine effort to make amends with you, then you can think about letting them back into your life. You may never be comfortable with this person again and that is okay.

While you shouldn't hold the past so transparently over either of your heads, you also should not forget. Your trust has been broken and it is not on you to fix it if you aren't (or never will be) ready. If you find yourself dwelling on the subject, remind yourself that you have done nothing wrong and there is no issue in needing to protect yourself from someone who already has a less than charitable history with you.

Key Takeaways

- Overthinkers tend to project their own negative self-image onto others. This is unfair to both the overthinker and to the other person.

- This projection can lead someone to sabotage a relationship, thus solidifying the self-fulfilling prophecy they made up.

- How you think other people perceive your relationships can corrupt what should be a wonderful thing because we tend to take the opinions of even total strangers as gospel.

- Because people can have such a negative influence both on how we see ourselves and discourage us from improvement, it is not unwarranted to cut a person off.

- You will be pressured and even gaslit by others to preserve a relationship that has run its course. You need to keep them from causing you to doubt your instincts.

- Forgiveness does not have to be for the sake of another person's feelings; it can be a tool to remove their power over you.

MASTERING YOUR EMOTIONS

"Worrying does not take away tomorrow's troubles. It takes away today's peace."

- RANDY ARMSTRONG

Rumination is not just a noisy brain; it can severely impact your emotional regulation. You are constantly brooding, doubting, and checking every choice you make and every interaction you have. We have a lot to keep track of in our daily lives, and by the time we finish all the boring stuff, we are often at a loss for what to do. Our free time is a precious commodity, and we may worry about the best way to spend it. Ultimately, we might make a snap decision, look for instant gratification, or just shut down and bury ourselves in our phones. We become spectators in our lives and then wonder why we are unhappy.

Streamlining your thoughts can go a long way to improving your overall disposition because you will have more bandwidth to dedicate to the things that really matter. But how can you do this? Most advice out there amounts to a minimalist lifestyle, keeping a journal, waking up earlier, and even finding God. While some of these things work for certain people, they are not for everyone. You are not busted if you can't wake up at five in the morning or keep a consistent journal. However, there are some exercises and tips you can carry out, so you have more of a foundation for your day-to-day life. Essentially, you are front-loading a lot of brain power in a few exercises so you don't have to think in the heat of the moment. You don't have to think about how to spend your day off because you know what you value; investing in that can never be a waste of time. It should be noted, though, that one of your core values should be self-care, and an important part of that is rest. Do not be pressured to fill every second of the day with activity. You will never reach your potential if you constantly burn out.

What Do You Want?

What is your dream in life? Is it a job, an object, or a physique? These are good starting points, but the real question is, what is the way of life that you aspire to? As you have aged into adulthood, you might have compromised five year old you's hopes and dreams. That version of you might have wanted to be a doctor, an astronaut, a zookeeper, or even just rich. Life happens, and you most likely are none of the things you thought you would be. Still, that doesn't mean you are a failure as long as you have a vision for how you want to live. Just because you are a data analyst instead of a firefighter does not mean you will inherently live a life full of regret.

So, ask yourself again, what kind of person do you want to be? Now for the cold bucket of ice water–are you actually living in a way that drives you closer to that ideal? You might not even have an answer to this question because you are busy working for others. When was the last time you did something because you wanted to? Not because a manager told you or because you felt societal pressure. When did you last feel immense pride in something not attached to a paycheck? Most of us don't think of our days beyond work. The rat race can completely erase your identity beyond being a good worker bee. It's time to take full account of your life.

The Eisenhower Matrix is a time management exercise where you can organize your whole to do list in order of importance, but in the process, you actually map out your priorities (*The Eisenhower Matrix*, 2017). When you look at the finished product, you may be depressed to see where you spend the majority of your time.

- **Important and Urgent**- These are tasks with deadlines that have consequences if they are not completed. Things like bills, professional projects, and assignments go here.
- **Important and Not Urgent**- This box is for personally important tasks, but there are no concrete consequences if you don't complete them. Essentially, your life stays the same

instead of improving if these are ignored. Applying for a new job, a fitness goal, and setting up an appointment can have a home here.

- **Not Important but Urgent**- Think of these as mundane maintenance tasks. Even though they're deemed as not important, if they are allowed to pile up, they can become a disaster. Miscellaneous paperwork, taking out the trash, and other such chores can go here.

- **Not Important and Not Urgent**- These tasks can only be deemed personally valuable and have no consequences if neglected. Calling a friend, getting into a new hobby, tackling a passion project, and meditation fit into this category.

Important and Urgent	Important and Not Urgent
Estimated time:	Estimated time:
Not Important but Urgent	Not Important and Not Urgent
Estimated time:	Estimated time:

Is a lot of your time being filled with things you do to survive instead of live? It's okay to feel a certain kind of way about it. You only know yourself in the context of working for someone else and may have lost track of the things that will make you feel whole.

Getting Your Priorities Straight

Now that you have an objective sense of where your life is headed, it's time for some self-reflection. If you like the direction you are going, then that's fantastic! Doing this exercise is still worth it, especially if you are in a good place. If the matrix results gave you a sense of existential dread, you need to sit down and think about your values. While your circumstances may change, people mostly retain their core values throughout their adult lives (Russo et al., 2022). As you grow, change jobs, and move, your values will always be there to guide you in moments of indecisiveness and chaos. Some good questions to ask yourself would be:

- If I never had to work again, what would I do with my time?
- If I could develop one skill, what would it be?
- How would I want a person to describe me to a stranger?
- What are five adjectives I would want to describe myself as?
- How would I know if I reached my full potential?
- What are my biggest fears right now?

- Is there something holding me back from reaching my goals?
- What do I keep telling people I am going to do?
- What was the last thing that made me truly happy (not just content)?

You might notice some themes emerge. Those are your values. You might find that you want to be more creative, help the community, advance your career, or have a specific lifestyle you aim for. They don't have to be extravagant; they just have to align with a life that will make you happy. Now look at your matrix; the things you do to reflect these values will be in the unimportant, not urgent box. While this category sounds frivolous, that box gives color to our lives. That is also the box you have probably neglected the most. Despite these things being your core values, you may not be living in a way that does them justice, and this can be a hard thing to see or accept.

Say you value making others happy and enjoy cooking; you would think that you would make time to learn recipes to challenge yourself and see people smile when they taste them. You might be so overwhelmed with life that you may not have the energy to try a new recipe, take a cooking class, shop for ingredients, or hone your skills. Because your skills have stagnated, you might find yourself doubting your abilities, so you stay in your comfort zone and might even have anxiety about cooking for others.

Getting Rid of the Mental Junk Drawer

You need to streamline your everyday thoughts to create room for more productive beliefs. We all have big goals and ideas, but they are being crowded by:

- mental lists
    - groceries
    - shows you want to catch up on
    - important dates
- the influence of ads.
- if you did your daily routine.
- bills.
- keeping up with friendships.
- every hobby you want to try.
- what you want to wear.
- your daily work and home tasks.
- general worry and self-doubt.
- and many more.

Your brain has a finite amount of resources to give to any topic, and the most immediate needs (food, shelter, instant gratification) tend to bubble up to the surface. As a result, we may say that we will dedicate a certain amount of time to something for our benefit, but it goes on the back burner, and we forget about it until the day is done and we haven't accomplished anything. Worse still, we dedicate more energy than we should to decisions that seem significant at the moment but are ultimately inconsequential. You need to limit sources of rumination that can affect your mood and productivity.

There are so many moving parts to our lives; keeping track of it without a system can lead to mental fatigue, burnout, and frustration. Since we tend to avoid things that make us uncomfortable until it turns into a fire, suddenly, even the simple things are ignored. Keeping a plant alive is an example.

The act is easy: water the plant, give it some store-bought nutrients, change the pot once it outgrows it, and let the sun do the rest. One day though, you forget about the plant, and when you suddenly realize it exists, it has started to wilt. Some people take the lesson and always remember to water their green friend. Others may now dread looking at the plant because they are ashamed of such a blatant example of their neglect. Instead of saving the plant by being sure to dedicate 30 seconds to watering it daily, they continue ignoring it until the plant is mummified. Automating, creating a simple routine, and visual cues such as a list are beneficial (Ludwig, n.d.).

Automating specific tasks is one of the best ways to declutter your mind. This isn't financially or technologically possible for everyone, but it helps with stress once the bills come. If you have a handle on your finances and can make more than a minimum payment, setting your bills to autopay will remove the dread of looking at the bill, signing in online, and paying it. You don't need to create a schedule, set a reminder, or panic when you realize it is past the due date and have to pay the penalty (Wise, 2017).

Another habit you should get into is making simple decisions ahead of time. While picking out clothes or creating a daily schedule seems simple at first blush, their frequency, and the number of choices you have can paralyze you in the moment. If you pick out clothes in the morning, you risk compromising your professional appearance because you are late or forgetful. You might only find out too late that you are out of clean underwear, none of your socks match, or that the shirt you wanted to wear needs to be pressed.

If you took five minutes to pick out an outfit in peace the night before, you might catch these things and devise an alternative. Another tedious decision is what we want to eat. Instead of dwelling on it, look at your fridge and see what you have and what you need. Decide right then and there what meals you are going to prepare that week. Write that on a whiteboard and keep it on the fridge. With your guidance and a visible plan (do not rely on memory, no matter how small the list is), you can shop for only what you need and avoid impulse buys.

The Planner Trap

Planners are a great tool, but they are often treated as the be all and end all of organized life. In the self-improvement space, planners are one of the most ubiquitous methods. Influencers dedicate careers to having an impeccable planner and the perfect pens, stickers, highlighters, and organizing systems to design more content centered around planners. They come in all shapes and sizes and can be digital or physical. They work for some people and situations, but for many people, they end up abandoned in a hard drive or smashed at the bottom of a bag.

For the overthinker, their mantra might as well be "the road to hell is paved with good intentions" (Martin, n.d.). The overthinker decides to adopt a new habit to help them get out of their way, but that habit becomes an overthinking sink. Seeing everything in black and white is a common distortion, so a person will stress if their planner is not right for them. Not only that, but is it neat enough? Should they add trackers? If so, what kind? Is it worth keeping if it's not neat? What if they forget to use it for a few days? Will the blank sheets bother them? These are all things that can become an anchor to progress.

Online, the bullet journal community takes planners to the next level. Their journals double as planners, including habit trackers such as water drinking, diet, exercise, etc. It can be tracked if it can be quantified on an aesthetically pleasing page. These journals are hot around New Year's since they are an accessible way to change your life and track your resolution progress. These journals require much planning, outlining, and organizing ahead of time–everything the overthinker is terrible at. Now not only do you have to keep up with your habits, but you have to make an effort to document them. Your failure to track for a few days may lead to frustration because your neglect ruins the journal you spent so much time organizing. These frustrations might bleed into the habit itself and compromise it as well. The mistake some overthinkers make is thinking that something is better because it requires more effort. Ultimately, all this effort does is overcomplicate things and add more clutter to your brain.

This is not to say that planners and even bullet journaling are bunk. There are entire communities of people that swear by them, but they are not the only way to hold yourself accountable. If you are going to have a planner, it should solve one general problem, like your inability to remember appointments and birthdays. It also needs to be easy to carry and access at all times. A large ornate planner is probably not the best idea, no matter how satisfying it is to open. Digital planners are a fantastic tool though they also have drawbacks. There is a lack of object permanence to them since they only exist in an app; you might not be able to access it if your phone has no power or signal, and your phone is a natural distractor that you have to get through whenever you need to jot something down ("Time Management and ADHD," n.d.).

You may need to try several planners and systems to see what sticks, but the results can be worth it.

Instead of trackers and planners, try simple visual cues. If you have a routine that varies daily, such as a skincare routine, write the schedule on a whiteboard or note it and put it on your bathroom mirror. To stop your head from spinning, it's not about developing a better memory, it's about taking your brain out of the equation entirely. Visual cues and reminders will keep you focused on the things you want to do while a bit of planning takes care of the boring stuff.

Keeping Roadblocks in Mind

We all have an ick that gets us procrastinating on certain tasks. They can range from the abstract to a fear of disappointment or the consequences of procrastination, or they can be as simple as a sensory issue. Things like being disgusted by touching wet food can keep dishes in the sink for days. You need to fix this before you incubate a new pandemic in your sink. The point is to get your task done without undoing consequences such as fees, a scolding, or roaches in your sink. There is no right or wrong way so long as your to-do list is accomplished with your sanity intact.

Prep is a must to limit resistance, especially if you have a brief window of motivation. A mantra or mindfulness exercise in your toolkit will help with more abstract barriers.

- This has to be done; the outcome will not change if I keep putting things off.
- Whatever happens, I can deal with it.
- This feeling will not go away until I deal with it.
- While the best time to start was a while ago, the second best time is right now.
- It is important for me to live in a clean space.
- I will feel better once all this work is done.

Your workspace must be catered to run with as few steps as possible (we will get back to this later). You may need to buy a couple of aids to deal with sensory issues. Dish gloves or nitrile gloves can be great if you are a germaphobe whose procrastination and anxiety are paradoxically making your living space dirtier. Using a facemask to deal with smells or even working in dim light can also help.

If you can't see it or smell the worst of it, you should be able to power through particularly nastier jobs without dry heaving. Of course, the best way to prevent this is to keep up with a consistent cleaning schedule. However, we all slip up or let our anxiety get the better of us. Having a plan when reaching a low point is a valid objective.

A Clear Space for a Clear Mind

Our spaces reflect our mental state. If your space is cluttered, your mind is as well. Healing the mind through your living space has been a concept for thousands of years, namely in the Chinese philosophy of "Feng Shui". By arranging your furniture, removing unnecessary clutter, and allowing light into a room, there is a belief that you can improve energy flow. The backbone of Feng Shui is the Taoist philosophy of yin and yang. The idea is not to erase opposing forces, as it is seen as a necessary force of nature; it is to balance the two forces (*The Science of Feng Shui*, n.d.). The same idea should apply to your space; the objective should not be an empty space but an efficient space.

Over the last few years, minimalism has been a trend amongst influencers. However, a sterile living area is often not the answer and can even harm an overthinker. Our possessions can inspire us and make us happy; that should not be forsaken just because someone on the internet said that clutter of any kind is bad. For overthinkers, cleaning is not just a matter of disinfecting; it is about getting rid of the build-up of daily life that can become a source of dread. If you are at home, look around. Do you see any of the following?

- A stack of mail that needs attention.
- Clothes that are either dirty or clean and just not put away.

- Empty containers that are crowding your surfaces.
- Objects that are scattered because they don't have a home.
- Things that you have not used in years such as clothes, electronics, or supplies.
- Things that are broken that you have been "meaning to fix".
- Boxes that you have no idea what the contents are.

If you have these, a deep clean might be needed. While this may seem monumental, it becomes more bearable and even fun if you approach it as a series of smaller tasks. Like Maria earlier, you may find yourself at your wits end because you constantly switch from task to task, resulting in negligible progress in many tasks instead of tangible progress in a few areas (which one do you think will motivate you more?). You should do your best to stick to one room at a time, even if it means closing the door so you cannot see the rest of the house (do not do this with cleaning chemicals).

Still, a room can have several tasks all pulling your mind in different directions; for this, you can try "junebugging". This is a common tactic in the ADHD world. How it works is, you pick a main task you want to accomplish, such as putting away laundry. If you have walked away from your task, drop what you are doing and return to the laundry; keep doing this until that main task is done. Don't beat yourself up for getting distracted or committing yourself to the new task. Go with the natural push and pull of your attention and guide it, do not stifle it. Soon your main task, and possibly a few others, will be done (Griffith, 2020).

Working Rewards into the Tedious Stuff

Cleaning is not everyone's idea of a fun weekend, but for a clear mind, it's got to be done. It does not need to be a joyless affair where all you have is the scent of cleaning chemicals to keep you company. You can motivate yourself to do a lot of things through fun rituals that happen while you do the hard work. Your mother might have already done this when she let the oldies blast through the house to let you know she was on a cleaning rampage. If you don't have the same passive aggressive streak as your dear mother, this can include listening to a podcast or audiobook while you clean and organize. It has to be something that will occupy your mind and has some anticipation, so you look forward to doing it. You have effectively reframed that task into something much more palatable.

These rituals will also help your brain shift into work mode. It may not seem like it, but task switching can burden the brain (*Why Is Task Switching so Hard?*, n.d.). If you cannot shift those mental gears, you may have this unnerving experience where you do not fully control your body because you cannot break the hold of what you are currently doing. Examples include:

- Scrolling through social media even though you know you are awake and already late to work.
- Working through your lunch despite your growling stomach pleading for you to stop.
- Fussing over a minute detail instead of moving on to another step.
- Sitting on an exercise machine and looking through social media instead of starting your next set.

By introducing consistent enjoyable rituals and rewards (they don't need to come after you have completed your to-do list), you allow your brain to adjust to the change gradually instead of attempting to shock it. You can associate special snacks, playlists, and even places with work. Just because hard work and maintenance is often not exactly glamorous, does not mean you can't inject a little bit of color into the experience.

Maximizing Your Space to Its Full Potential

Caring for your possessions is the best way to motivate them to support you, their owner. When you treat your belongings well, they will always respond in kind.

- Marie Kondo

Rita was stoked to be at her new lab job. She had completed her training and was ready to start experiments. Since Rita was new, she was sticking with techniques that she had done in the past, especially since everyone else was at a long meeting and would be unavailable for most of the day if she had questions. She had a list of things to do, podcasts set, and a heart full of ambition to prove herself. She took a cursory glance at her new bench seeing she had pipettes, tubes, and racks that were all hers to use.

She went to print out her protocol to check against when she realized the file name looked identical to the other 20, she had downloaded because she did not bother to rename them or put them in a specific folder. After 10 minutes of searching, she finally found what she needed. With that out of the way, she could get to the hard science. She started her experiment, and it was going well until she realized that she had forgotten to defrost a delicate reagent and neglected to preheat an incubator. She was set back a half hour. No problem, she could grab a cup of coffee and get back to it later.

Setback after setback plagued Rita. She had to stop and get up to look for more tubes because she neglected to ensure she had enough. She had to get up and get more reagents several times because she did not account for how many samples she had to process. She had to search constantly, and she did not want to interrupt an important meeting so she could ask where she could get another box of pipette tips. This would have taken her an hour in her old lab, but as she was in a new space and anxious about impressing, hours were added to her work. Rita was at her wit's end, and the last straw was when she could not find where the gels were kept to run her samples. They were on a high shelf, and when she struggled to get them down, the box fell, and individual gels were scattered everywhere. Rita did something she had not done since her university days; she cried in the lab. Had she taken the time to take inventory, optimize her space, and prepare based on her protocol, she would have gotten her work done efficiently and had time to go out and grab a poke bowl for lunch. Instead, she was frustrated, starving, and doubting her abilities in the lab.

We all hate fetch quests, but when you share a space or are just plain disorganized, they can become a repetitive and frustrating fixture of your life. You have no idea what you have if you are prepared for the day ahead. You already have people interrupting your flow; the last thing you need is to bring more speed bumps by being disorganized. Whether it's at your job or your home, some simple rules can keep you focused on doing what you want instead of looking for things.

Sparking Joy by Harnessing Your Inner Marie Kondo

Your space is so clean it's sparkling. You feel pride and like a weight has been lifted from your shoulders. Without the chanting of "I should really clean" constantly in your ears, suddenly you can switch gears and finally think about something else. Having a clean workspace is only one part of the equation. Now you need to optimize it for all your needs. You will find many opinions and Pinterest boards on organizing in a way that facilitates being productive. Many of them can miss the mark, as being optimized is only the second most important part of this equation. Honestly, the most vital part is that you like the space you will inhabit. This is why minimalism is not for everyone. Some people like working in a place resembling an Apple store rather than a creative hub, but chances are, you want something with more personality.

You probably have things taking up valuable real estate that you haven't even thought about in years. Before you indiscriminately start tossing things, really put some thought into what you want to keep. Downsizing is a vital part of this process.

You should ask yourself two questions:

- *Do I really need this?*
- *Does this stir an emotion in me?*

When cleaning, Kondo advises that you lay out all your possessions to visualize how much you have accumulated. That iPhone box and drawer filled with obsolete phone chargers that date back to the Bush administration can be trashed. Clothes that have not seen daylight in years, if they are in good shape, can be donated; if not, they have to go. You may also realize you have stacks of old records that need to be organized rather than put away and photos that need sorting. By now, you might feel a lot of shame and frustration at how cluttered your life has become.

Becoming a packrat is a natural consequence of overthinking. You can tune into an episode of Hoarders to see this for yourself. People insist that actual garbage has a place in their life and cannot let anything go. While you are probably not living in a house with magazine stacks up to the ceiling, you might insist that you will regret letting something out of your sight. It's your brain catastrophizing the simple act of downsizing, and it will make you rationalize keeping your 30-gallon bin of scuffed and matted My Little Pony figurines that have not seen the light of day since the 1990s. Your worst-case scenarios are entirely illogical.

In reality, you probably will not even miss the things you choose to part with in a week. But still, the threat of regret will trump the fact that you might run out of room in your home every time. Only when you realize that you might outgrow your space do you realize something has to change.

This is why you must ask yourself if an object "sparks joy", or at least an emotion that is not needless anxiety. Our possessions can remind us of a better time, inspire us, or make us smile. A plant has no practical value in your space, but the touch of life they add to any space is proven to boost your mood (Yeo, 2021). The Kondo method states that you should pick up an object and examine how you feel while you hold it. If you have an emotional reaction, it's worth keeping; if not, consider discarding it. If that seems wasteful, you can do your best to donate what you have, but you should be careful. You should only donate something that you would be happy to buy yourself. Also, when you set aside donated goods, try to have a way to stay accountable, or else it will just end up taking up space again, which defeats the whole point of the exercise. Another option would be saving money on rags and cutting up your old garments to clean up all spills. Either way, they are no longer in your closet, and you are left with clothes you are actually excited to wear. You won't waste time picking through something you would never wear anyway.

Sometimes it's not a matter of if you should throw something out, but where it should be stored. The occasional pop vinyl is great on a desk, but are you constantly knocking it over or staring into its beady, soulless eyes? Maybe your direct line of sight in a place where you need to be concentrating is not the best place for it. Consider dedicating a shelf near your desk to the things that make you happy.

It would be best if you used logic when it comes to how you put things away. Color coding or going by size or aesthetic are okay, but they don't consider the human factor, i.e., how often you use something. Everything you use daily should be out in the open or easily accessible and easy to see. Your stuff should not just be utilitarian, it should inspire you, but it cannot do that if it's forgotten in the dark. You would never store your table salt on the top shelf of your cabinet, right? This makes all that daily maintenance way more effortless. It keeps you using the things you want if you have object permanence issues. No more suddenly remembering you spent money on a nice cologne or perfume only for it to languish in the back of a cabinet.

Everything you own should have a place it lives. You should not have to search for anything from the remote to the extra toilet paper. Dividers and containers can make even the most cluttered space nice and organized. Things going into long-term storage should go into labeled clear containers so you can keep track of what you have without grabbing a ladder, taking down the box, and physically opening it. You want every aspect of your life to be as easy as possible. If you know where things are, nothing should ever get lost, and you don't have to think about where the best place to put something is because you already know. Organizing becomes more passive and less of a burden.

Finally, you should consider some more out-of-the-box accommodations. A cleaning cart you can easily wheel into every room instead of going underneath your sink; grabbing a cleaner, and realizing you forgot to grab the ScrubDaddy can make cleaning much more efficient. It should have everything you need and, since it will be more visible, you can easily see if you are running low on anything to avoid derailing your cleaning day. Also, consider having little containers to drop wrappers and other dry garbage in (no food or bodily fluids, please) all over your house. Sometimes if there is so much garbage across the room, we forget and just set trash down, and there it will stay until we take a look and realize our home has scattered litter everywhere. At least then, all you have to do is dump the containers once when they get full instead of bending down to pick up every bit of scrap (Kondo, 2014).

Key Takeaways

- Mastering emotions takes organization of both your priorities and physical space.

- Getting a sense of what you want in your life can help you stop ruminating on why something might not feel fulfilling. It is easier to plan ahead when you have a clear vision.

- The Eisenhower matrix, while a great time management tool, can also help you map where your time is going.

- An efficient space makes for an efficient mind. Some solutions may seem silly, but if it helps you to remember things, then they aren't so stupid.

- The best way to organize the important things in your mind is to take them out of there entirely. Visibility and deciding ahead of time when emotions aren't so charged should become routine.

SETTING YOURSELF UP FOR SELF-GROWTH

"The very best thing you can do for the whole world is to make the most of yourself."

- WALLACE WATTLES

When we think of wealth and success, we think of people like Warren Buffet. He is the godfather of modern investing. The man has made 60 billion dollars through shrewd investments that, without the gift of hindsight, seemed like a risk. He is constantly giving talks and making the TV rounds, giving his opinion on the economy while everyone else in the finance world hangs on to every word he says. He is known as a funny and engaging storyteller when giving speeches. You would never think someone like him would have been afraid of anything. The truth is, Warren Buffet suffered from crippling stage fright early in his career.

Buffet was a natural investor and probably would have had a lucrative career in the stock trade regardless of his bashfulness in front of a crowd. He knew he would never reach his full potential (larger than life) if he did not become more assertive in public. The level of influence he has could never be accomplished in the shadows. He had to step into the light and become the face of his ideas. Warren knew he needed help, so he enrolled in a public speaking class to confront his fear. There he was surrounded by people who had similar struggles. Knowing he was not alone in his shyness gave him a sense of comfort. He was so successful he started his investing class, where Buffet was instructing people in their forties when he was still a kid in his early twenties.

Warren Buffet became one of the most influential people in the modern world by having the humility and introspection to identify a weakness. His experiences can teach us a valuable lesson regarding self-growth; leaning on others and getting uncomfortable is the only way to break out of our shells (Thompson, 2020).

You have been making great strides in managing your emotions, so much so that you are ready to challenge yourself. What big projects have you had in your brain for years? Do you want to oil paint, learn to code, or take up baking? Is it a lifestyle change such as getting fit or a finance goal? For this exercise, let's say you want to write a book. You have had an idea rolling around in your head for over a decade, but you always felt awkward committing it to the written word. For years you have thought your story is embarrassing; you don't know how to write, and everyone will laugh at you and judge you if they find out. You now have the tools to deal with those cognitive distortions so you can step onto the stage. However, there are still many obstacles to overcome in actually doing the thing. You need to be thoughtful to set yourself up for success.

Why Do Most Lofty Goals Fail?

In the early 2000s, reality TV was obsessed with extreme transformations. We loved watching the fairy tale of an average Joe or a plain Jane being whisked away by a TV executive, having their life turned upside down, and emerging with a new lease on life (and $50,000). It was the fantasy of your average TV viewer, as these participants didn't need to think or hold themselves accountable, at the cost of their privacy; they had a whole team dedicated to helping them make the changes. These people at the time thought getting selected was a blessing, but in reality, it was a nightmare.

What the suits did not tell them was that the network was not invested in their lives at all, they wanted to make content that would inspire millions at home to watch their show, become invested, then buy all the products and services shilled either in the show or during a commercial break. The contestant had unwittingly become a pawn in the reality show game and would be subject to unhealthy, unproven means of treatment in the name of entertainment. It also fueled the intense attitudes towards weight loss and change in general that plague our culture today.

SETTING YOURSELF UP FOR SELF-GROWTH

Resolutions are a tale as old as time. Whether it's because of a New Year, an epiphany, or a scare, we have all decided at one point that we are going to change our lives completely right then and there. We buy everything we need, set up memberships, and consume a lot of quick content to inspire us. Most people do well starting. In the case of New Year's resolutions, though, 80% fail by February. Why can't we just stick to things? The desire is there, we have strong motivators, and we seem to be in a place where we should be able to improve our lives.

The main issue stems from the vagueness of our goals. How many resolutions have we seen that amount to straightforward phrases?

- *I am going to lose weight/get stronger/get healthier.*
- *I am going to be a better worker/spouse/parent.*
- *I am going to be more creative.*
- *I am going to take better care of myself.*

While the spirit is there, these are aspirational outcomes rather than process-focused outcomes. Someone might say they are going to lose weight, but how? What is their plan? Are they looking to build muscle and get into cardio? What kind of diet are they going to follow? Have they spoken to a doctor? These are all considerations that need to be addressed before committing. Instead, people haphazardly follow random dieting advice from an unqualified influencer in their 20s and sign up for a gym. They buy fitness watches, trackers, supplements, planners, new clothes, and water bottles in the hopes that these things will motivate them to stick to the plan. The problem is that they neglect the most important thing; they have to consider their current lifestyle and personality when executing their goals initially.

Our minds become polluted with all or nothing thinking and a lack of direction. Consequently, we become addicted to the idea of change rather than the actual process. We see the destination rather than the long winding journey and tend not to pay attention to potential roadblocks that may lie ahead.

- A natural night owl will likely fail to get up at 5 a.m. to finish some writing before work.
- A person who loves bread will not be able to easily pivot into keto.
- Someone who is sedentary is probably not ready for the amount of will they experience after the first workout when they inevitably overdo it.

Yes, some people can quit smoking cold turkey; but overthinkers are often not among those people. The key to change is sustainability. You may not be able to sustain a strict, low-fat, low-carb diet in your first week. This is where people start to get cravings, give in, and instead of taking stock of what went wrong, fall back into their old ways.

Planning Around Success

Just because the planning stage is addictive does not mean we can't still have fun with it. Since we fall in love with the idea of a goal rather than the work it takes to achieve it, we need to see if we can tolerate going through the process. If our book is an ambitious fantasy, jumping into it can lead to frustration if the author hates world-building or designing magic systems. There is a certain order you have to go through for your project to make sense and remain attainable.

If you have ever been in awe of an artist sketching a beautiful form, you are neglecting the fact that this person had to start with learning shapes, studying human anatomy, learning shadowing and getting the hang of perspective; all things that probably took years to master. This is where dipping your toes in classes and groups can come in handy.

This does not mean you need to pay exorbitant money for private coaching. You can commit to trying one class to see if you connect with the instructor and their methods. You will be surrounded by like-minded people and potential mentors (put a pin in this) where you can laugh, share your projects, and commiserate over your struggles. You now have a low-stakes environment to learn and try out ideas, not to mention you will get a more accurate representation of the process.

You should decide how many resources you are willing to sink into this new adventure. Having a general budget is a good idea and you will be able to see how much disposable income you actually have. You might realize that if you tighten your belt in a few places, you can afford to spend a bit extra on a class or put some away for future purchases. It also keeps your feet firmly planted on the ground when a targeted ad comes your way in an attempt to get you to part with your money. If you try and guess how much you are willing to spend instead of doing the cold hard math, in a moment of doubt you might consider the whole thing a financial risk when it's not or start to overthink and decide you need better tools. Go by the numbers so you don't have to dwell on money.

You should also decide on a goal and how you plan to achieve it. If you want to be an artist, your goal is landscapes, comics, or figure drawing. If you are programming, do you want to build cool apps or be more efficient at your job? These are all important questions you need to answer before you spend a dime or make any sort of commitment. What does your schedule look like? Do you have the time and the energy to dive into the deep end or will this be a more part time endeavor? Also, what does progress look like to you? What milestones do you want to accomplish in a month or a year? Write out everything you need to do to get started and what skills you need to get a handle on or you might end up fighting yourself instead of enjoying the journey. When we are in the thick of it, we can often forget why we even started pursuing something. Write your inspiration on a post-it note and put it somewhere you can see it. That way you always have something of a beacon when the road ahead is clouded with doubt.

Paying For Your Lack of Vision

Image on the screen is a pristine looking barbeque pit.

"Ahh. Yeah, that's one fine-looking barbecue pit."
Cut to Homer's pathetic attempt at a DIY pit.
"Why doesn't mine look like that?"

- Homer Simpson, The Simpsons

Capitalism loves our addiction to planning. You will be peddled with classes, products, and plans that promise to motivate you and make your journey easier. You see yourself in the journeys of influencers who only show a sanitized version of their process. The dangerous part of the planning stage is that it's the easiest part. You need to plan effectively or you risk getting trapped on the plan treadmill.

Everything is still hypothetical; it can be kept to yourself so there are no real consequences if you fall off track. You are researching and buying everything you think you need to be successful at your goal. Companies know this is a vulnerable time for you and they can feed you ads based on your web searches. Hitting "add to cart" and the anticipation of opening your package gives us a dopamine hit and a sense of accomplishment. You cannot possibly fail in this novel stage, and it can be an addictive place to stay.

Now you have bought everything you think you need to fix your life. Maybe it's a fancy new program, books, kits, and a bucket of not only supplies, but the best supplies. After all, you don't want to be limited by cheap materials. The problem is, you might have done all of this without a specific goal or project in mind and you probably have no idea how to use half of the things you have bought. You go online only to discover you erroneously bought several things and you need to switch them out.

Or, more likely, the dopamine rush ends when you actually try to sit down and do the work. You are lacking in experience to accomplish what you want. You might get stressed out by the idea of ruining your fancy new supplies on a starter project and realize that maybe going cheap for your first attempt might not have been such a bad idea. Whether it's your anxiety around wasting your fancy supplies, realizing you don't like what you bought when you actually go to work with it, or the frustration of creating something that is objectively terrible, you might have ended up with boxes of abandoned supplies and broken dreams.

When you are starting something brand new, it is best to not sink so many resources into your first attempt. For one, you won't waste time researching specialized tools that you may never use or comparing brands. A simple web search of starter materials or asking someone at a craft store will probably yield you some good results. You also want to avoid the paralysis that comes with the risk of ruining something like a fancy sketchbook, canvas, or anything you deem permanent. It is natural to want to make something you are proud of, but the road to mastery is paved with some retrospectively embarrassing attempts. Keeping things simple and cheap also helps dull the novelty of your prospective craft. This is actually a good thing. You won't be so high off anticipation and crash when you realize that progress can be tedious.

Once you not only get the hang of your new hobby but can confirm that you like it and want to dedicate more time to it, then you can start investing more money into it. If you take a class, you can ask your instructor or peers for their recommendations and get feedback on your process, which may differ from that of your peers. Either way, once you commit some time, you know how you like to work, what frustrates you, and what your concrete goals are. Shopping will be much more worthwhile and efficient once you have a vision for what you think progress is, rather than swiping your credit card in the dark chasing a high.

Creating Your Battle station

If you are going to go out and do cool things, you need a battle station. A sanctuary where you can get messy, be creative, and let your mind loose with ideas. You cannot let your mind be crowded with thoughts of cleanliness, discomfort, or your other responsibilities. This is time you have set aside for yourself, and you will use it to its full potential. Your battle station will have everything you need for a given task within arm's reach. The principles for a fully optimized space will be on steroids here. You need a clear space to work, while at the same time having all your tools visible and accessible. Depending on what you plan on doing, this can mean storage space, overhead shelving, or power. It also needs to inspire you. If that means incorporating pictures of your family, cool lights, books that have inspired you, or action figures of people you aspire to be, go for it so long as they are not in the way. Make a battle station that your inner child would love.

Along with being practical, your battle station needs to be comfortable. If you start associating it with pain, both physical and mental, you will never use it. This means finding a comfortable chair, considering ergonomic accommodations, and even making sure the overhead lighting is not too harsh. You should look at this space and be excited to get to work there and it should make shifting into work mode easier.

This also applies to your digital space. If your work is more tech-based, having as few steps as possible between you and your goals should be a top priority. We simply do not interact with technology as we would with a physical object. Digital files are abstract and much easier to lose. You can become paranoid that you have deleted your thesis by accident, so you make backups on backups with minute differences in their names. How much time have you wasted looking for a specific file because your computer is a redundant disorganized mess? Default names can be a mishmash of numbers and letters and you need to make a conscious effort to rename and organize them. If you are reliant on your computer, you should take a day and practice the Kondo method there too.

If you are truly paranoid, you can make a backup of your computer and store it on an external drive. Otherwise, do you really need a 10 year old slideshow from your university days popping up when you try to search for something? Keep final versions of your projects and archive the rest.

To keep your peace of mind, create backups of your most important files and projects in both the cloud and a physical drive. It feels tangible. Feel free to clear out any old research, downloads, games you have not played in years, and photos of people you no longer speak to. Organize everything into folders with intuitive names. You may have noticed a pattern with decluttering, it involves front loading a lot of work. However, by making a day out of it instead of waiting for a crisis, you will save yourself a ton of grief in the future.

How to Keep Your New Hobby from Becoming a Nightmare

So, you have been working hard on your plan and are excited. The challenge is lighting up your brain in ways you never thought possible. You want to jump in and dedicate all of your waking hours to this new thing. But wait; you are not done setting the stage yet. You must devise ways to keep yourself from burning out before reaching your potential.

You should keep calm while starting out; not just in making sure not to take on too much at once, but also in paying attention to your mood. Trying something new, especially when you are on your own, can strain your brain. You can have the perfect plan, but the growing pains will still wear you down. It is a baptism of fire, but that does not mean you cannot make the process bearable. You can add calming factors such as aromatherapy while you work. Choosing music that calms you down or listening to a more upbeat podcast during more stressful moments can also help. If your particular hobby requires dexterity or intense concentration, a podcast describing how a serial killer chopped someone into a hundred pieces is probably not the best choice.

Finally, while it seems counterintuitive, you should set aside time for relaxation that does not involve any aspect of your hobby. You want to give your mind a break to pivot into rest mode. Not to mention, you always want to leave yourself wanting more. Have fun and change the flavors of your past times. If your big project is creative, don't be afraid to veg out on the couch or do a puzzle. If you are sitting all day, go outside and get your steps in. As painful as it sounds, peppy gym goers are that way for a reason. Movement releases dopamine, which puts you in a better mood and helps you sleep. If your goals have you thinking more academically, get creative with a low-stakes hobby like crocheting (beware, this can be quite the rabbit hole of yarn and patterns if you are not careful) or get into some trash reality television. We want to challenge our brains, not exhaust them.

It's Okay to Step Back

You may find yourself realizing that what you wanted to do is not a good fit. There will always be frustrations in trying something new, but if you cannot bear to look at your hobby or become overly anxious about it, then maybe it's time to take a break or stop altogether. By taking some distance, you can examine what went wrong. Perhaps you got bad advice, or a particular instructor was not a good fit. Or maybe it turns out your new fixation was not what you thought it would be. You can pivot how you approach this hobby or put it down altogether and come away with more knowledge and resourcefulness. There is no shame in not wanting to engage in something that has become nothing more than an energy sink. Life is too short for this.

Key Takeaways

- To make demonstrable change in your life, you need to take a step back and create a realistic plan.
- Goals that are overly ambitious and/or vague are doomed for failure.
- You need your goals to be attainable and gradual or you risk progress not sticking.
- The planning stage is a deceptively vulnerable one because it is exciting and easy; be sure not to stay there too long.
- Over-complicating goals will lead to burning out much faster.
- Remember to enjoy yourself and if it turns out this new way of life isn't for you, never be afraid to step back and pivot. So long as you are always learning and improving, you can never falter.

MANAGING THE
GROWING PAINS OF RISK

"Don't worry about failure. Worry about the chances you miss when you don't even try."

- SHERMAN FINESILVER

Jenny has had a book idea since she was a teenager. This idea was always precious to her but bringing it to life always scared her. Now she is in her thirties and has decided that she wants to try and put pen to paper and maybe even publish. Even if no one ever read it, she wanted to prove that she could create something that would last in this world.

There was only one problem; Jenny is an accountant who is excellent with math and spreadsheets, but when it comes to creative writing, she needs help. Every time she sat down to write her masterpiece, she was quickly overwhelmed. She learned quickly that having an idea is different from having a vision. Jenny struggled to get her story structure down, hone in on her characters' voices, and create a magic system that made sense. She had to constantly double back to make sure her story was consistent. Since Jenny picked an actual location, she realized that she had to do serious research on the setting so locals would not scoff if she got a detail wrong.

This left her depressed, as this project, which was supposed to be fun, became a chore. She felt embarrassed both at her progress and her idea. It got to the point where she could barely look at her notes. She had envisioned a romantic scene with her handwriting, her research, and making beautiful physical notes. She had bought all-new stationery, highlighters, pens, and colorful sticky notes. She soon realized that handwriting notes was time-consuming and made for a sore wrist. Not to mention how crazy it had started to make her having to track down every sheet of paper. She created several new writing journals, thinking that a clean slate would reset her mind and help her progress–she was wrong. She had made no progress despite putting hours of her life into this project.

She could always stop; no one knew she wanted to write, and she wasn't hurting for money. Other aspects of her life, such as cleaning her apartment and going to the gym, had also taken a back seat. But still, this would be the one thing in her life that she was doing for herself. She had made so much progress regarding overthinking at her job, but she was stuck when the stakes boiled down to an abstract sense of self-worth and the ability to grow. Jenny realized she was going about writing all wrong. She needed to optimize her time and planning so her brain would have more room for creativity, instead of defaulting back to anxiety.

Managing Your Time

You already have a plan for how long you will dedicate to your new hobby. However, this change in your schedule can throw you for a loop if you are not careful. Believe it or not, time blindness is a genuine phenomenon seen in people with ADHD, but it can happen to just about anyone who isn't paying attention. You may underestimate how much time you dedicate to the most basic things. If you enter a flow state, you may succeed too hard. You will start something in the morning, and the next time you look up, the sun is setting, and your day is gone. This isn't always a bad thing, but it can start messing with your other responsibilities. Do not try and guess how long you do things. You will end up overthinking it and be entirely off.

The only way to do this right is to be objective instead of relying on memory. Take a single day and track how long basic things take, such as brushing your teeth, cooking breakfast, commuting, walking the dog, etc. Get a rough estimate of where your time goes and how much you can spare. Be sure you have access to the time in all your main living areas. You may have a phone, but it is a potential distraction. A clock on the wall or a digital clock on the side is a much better option.

Getting Used to Living in Cold Executive Function

Remember how we mentioned all the way back in chapter one how some people need a fire lit under them to get things done? Well, if you are going to make long-term changes, this is not sustainable. Compared to hot executive function, which is emotionally driven, "cold executive function" is more planning-based. It's the ability to get things done without a ticking time bomb and is fueled by working memory and cognitive flexibility (Salehinejad et al., 2021). In short, you do something just because you should act in a timely manner.

Working under pressure may have turned you into a diamond, but you might need some time to recover once you finish something. Severe burnout cannot be fixed by a weekend in bed. Depending on how long you spend in crisis mode, it can take months to recover (*How Long Does It Take to Recover From Burnout?*, n.d.). You will lose momentum and will most likely regress if or when you return to your goal. An overactive brain hates cold executive function because it is boring. You have to make this state as pleasant and rewarding as possible.

Cold executive functions rely on retrieving memories and planning. As such, you have to put in the time to make a plan of attack for the day and keep track of your thoughts. If you don't, you will fizzle out. A plan makes it easier to maintain some cognitive flexibility, or your ability to switch tasks (remember when we discussed how difficult this could be?). It's everything you have had trouble with since you were in school. The cold executive functions waters may be less tantalizing than the hot executive functions pool. Still, mastering it can help you use your time effectively and avoid leaning on intense emotions to get things done.

The Power of The Almighty List

Everyone and their mother have advocated for lists. You can buy pretty list templates online and there are even whole planners dedicated to them. Why do people swear by them? The thing is, when used properly, they do work. Surgeons at the top of their field use lists, even if they have performed the surgery hundreds of times. Let the past relax you and take care of the future you, who might be more emotional and tired. Having to pick or remember something in the heat of the moment is a recipe for disaster. Have you ever had to pack for a vacation the day of? You are bound to forget something, and you better hope it is something you can buy later and not something catastrophic like medication. At the same time, you will end up over packing because you are now thinking about every worst-case scenario where you might need three raincoats and every pair of underwear you own.

Whatever you are planning for, as long as it's low stakes, write an objective list of what you will most likely need and do so ahead of time. Do not skip the listing process if you must do something last minute. Taking even a minute to take stock of a situation is better than going in half-cocked. In intensive care units, where stakes and emotions are as high as possible, medical teams still take a few seconds to stop and listen to a verbal handoff report. This gives them a first-hand account of what is happening and allows them to calm down and take in what they need to do.

Checklists are also a great motivational tool (Gawande, 2011). They allow you to see at a glance how much you have done for the day. Each item should represent the completion of a milestone or a completed task. Avoid oversimplifying them, or else they will lose their impact (there is one exception to this). You need to keep the dopamine rolling so your mind doesn't want to leave the wonderland of focus. It may seem silly, but that little check can refill your tank. It will also give you a tangible endpoint where your brain can disconnect from the project, and you can take a well-needed rest.

Start Small

If you are the type of person that gets intimidated by a large project, it would be in your best interest to break the ice with as little force as possible. That first brush stroke or opening paragraph are the most intimidating. You can become completely paralyzed at the thought of your project moving beyond the hypothetical, becoming subject to the possibility of failure. Your first action has to be simple, so you get through it and gain momentum. Let's say you are writing a thesis. You might find yourself procrastinating because the whole project becomes even more real once you begin. Anxiety fills your stomach with vomiting bees, and you are overthinking your first paragraph or even your first sentence. The problem isn't the paper, it's the knowledge that you are about to take on a giant undertaking. The first item on your checklist should be to just make the title page. For larger projects, if you can, put tasks in order of complexity. You will lay down good scaffolding and let your mind get used to the idea of a new activity. You will then have gained some experience, which leads to creativity.

Limit Interruptions

You have been working hard to master the flow state, but what about staying there? Interruptions are everywhere, and it's not even limited to your phone. Meetings, Slack pings, and other things in your environment will instantly rip you out of the zone. It takes 10 to 15 minutes to reach this state, so you will have to go through the whole process again. Offices are dystopian in their design in an attempt to increase productivity and team collaboration, but lately, they have gone backward. Open office settings are a blight on the ability to concentrate. Phones, meetings, chatty coworkers, the fact that your coworker keeps bringing fish for lunch. All these things have become your problem. Your home is even more distracting. When you know you want to work on something important, that sink full of dishes suddenly becomes more enticing. Maybe you have noisy neighbors who are too into swearing at their online game friends, or you have kids who demand your attention.

Having your work area face away from the rest of the living space like towards a wall or out a window is a great start. The only thing that exists is your desk. A good set of noise canceling headphones, or a white noise maker will dampen or even stop all ambient noise. You should have a ritual before you start that can include:

- Setting all devices to "do not disturb". This includes your laptop and tablet if they are integrated with your phone.
- If you are at work, block out your time on a calendar and make it clear you are using it for uninterrupted work.
- Setting up your space. That means making sure you have everything you need. You wouldn't start baking a cake if you didn't have flour, would you?

You also have to remember your potential roadblocks if your environment changes. Sometimes your home is the worst place to get work done. You might have a nosey family member in your business, noisy neighbors, endless temptations, or a less than reliable internet connection. Sometimes we need a change of scenery to get our minds in the right place for some work. A coffee shop is a great place to get some work done on the computer. The calming ambiance, caffeine, and being surrounded by other people reading or tapping away at their keyboards create the perfect energy for productivity. Unfortunately, you are now in an environment you cannot control, and some scenarios can completely derail you. You know, once your momentum is gone, there is no getting it back. Plus, do you really want to pay for another cup of coffee to obtain permission to sit down at another coffee shop?

The most likely roadblocks are hunger, uncomfortable temperatures, inaccessible bathrooms, and lack of power sources. Be sure to either eat before you go, pack a snack, or have the money to buy something on the road. Hunger is not conducive to top notch work, and the last thing you need is to have a stomach ache. This goes for hydration as well. Still, with water comes the call of the toilet. First, bathroom access can differ between a full day in the zone and leaving after an hour because there is no bathroom. The potty dance can also lead to mistakes because you cannot concentrate on the task when your brain is screaming at you to go pee.

There is also temperature. Places can either be too hot or cold, and that can make working unpleasant. Finally, there is power. It's not just your laptop you have to worry about, though. That is a huge concern if your work is digital. There is also your phone if you need to navigate or use music to minimize distractions. If these lose power, your day is likely to be shot. Having to deal with the ambient noise of screaming children and obnoxious adults will kill your motivation and have you seeking the safety of your home, especially if you suffer from sensory overload.

The best way to combat this is to return to your list and, if need be, have a dedicated bag where you keep duplicates of your most essential items. Useful chargers are the one thing you should hoard like a dragon. Ask for them as gifts, buy one if you get a little extra income, and get your hands on enough that they can stay plugged in or in a bag. You can't stress about forgetting a charger if they are everywhere. Plus, you will always be someone else's hero when they forget their phone charger because they keep forgetting.

Keeping Your Head in The Game

Keeping up with mindfulness can help you through that initial hump of your new endeavor. We have already discussed positive affirmations, but there is a deeper level to delve into. Emile Coue surmised that we could practice "autosuggestion" to guide our thoughts (Coue, 1920). In short, you can hypnotize yourself into staying focused and not ruminating without a hypnotist that might also make you cluck like a chicken. It is similar to the placebo effect where a person feels better without intervention, because they believe they did something to improve. While there are charlatans pitching cures based on this effect, the science behind it is no joke and it's free of charge. Your brain is a wonderful thing and so long as it is convinced of something, it can make it real to an extent. Affirmations are part of autosuggestion, but they are not the whole picture. Autosuggestions are more about challenging your whole mindset to achieve long term goals.

Your suggestions need to use positive and decisive language. You have to crowd out the *I can't* musings with *I will*. There is no room for doubt here. There are no limits. If you want to become a CEO, you need to repeat that desire back to yourself, even if people would laugh at the ascertain. You should never frame your suggestions around a negative emotion. Phrases like "I don't want to be a loser" or "I hate my body" will only serve to poison your mind. Remember, improvement is an act of self-love, not a punishment for your perceived shortcomings.

Actions have to take place in the present. You will sign up for this class now. You will start that diet today. If you leave an inch of wiggle room, the devil on your shoulder will take a mile. There needs to be a sense of urgency for your actions to be guided by autosuggestion. To prime your mind to accept the fact that you can change, your suggestions be framed as if you have already succeeded in your goal. "I am proud of how hard I worked to start my own successful business" or "I have reached my fitness goals and I feel fantastic" are good templates to start out with (Sweeney, n.d.).

Unlike a positive affirmation, which can be done on the go, autosuggestion is best achieved if you are in a relaxed state. You need a place that is comfortable and free of distractions so you can enter into a hypnotic trance. Hopefully after some Trataka candle gazing, you've gotten the hang of entering that state of concentration.

By simply coming to the conclusion that you are a successful person, you might feel your luck changing. It is not your imagination. We split the world into haves and have nots. There are those that fall upward and trip into every opportunity one could ever ask for, then there are the people that can't seem to ever catch a break. While it might be comforting to resign yourself to a life of bad luck, it might just come back to behavior. People that seem to have the luck factor, might just be confident. They follow their instincts, network, and prepare for success rather than failure. They aren't afraid to take chances because they know they will be alright in the end and can spin any shortcoming into a lesson or victory. Changing your mindset can change how the whole world seems to interact with you.

Keep An Idea Parking Space

Picture this: you are writing a book and you are on a roll with supplying helpful information to the masses. Suddenly, you are struck with a bolt of inspiration, something in your life that can make for a great anecdote that readers can connect with. You scroll up to figure out where to place this bold new idea when you forget what you were going to write. Fine, you will go back to what you are doing, except you lost the plot on that page too. Now you have nothing to write. This oddly specific but not at all based on reality situation demonstrates how ideas sometimes need to be put away, instead of fleshed out right away. All it will do is interrupt your momentum and put the whole writing session in jeopardy.

As soon as something pops into your head like an idea for a great Christmas gift, the solution to how you are going to solve a structure issue in your latest novel, or something you need to buy, write it down. It can be in a notepad, a dedicated notes section on your phone, your skin, or even on a napkin (just don't throw it out). First, the act of writing something will make it more likely that you won't forget it. Second, you have taken this idea out of your head. This way you do not need to rack your brain and get frustrated if the thought was fleeting. Your ideas deserve better than to be locked away in the inner recesses of your brain.

Reward Yourself

We have already discussed rewarding ourselves during a task, but it is vital also to give kudos after a full day of work or after completing a particular milestone. It can be as simple as ordering your favorite meal or treating yourself to a few episodes of your favorite binge-worthy TV show. Remember, while abstract motivators are acceptable, nothing beats a tangible prize for a job well done. Hell, even if you end your day in a bad mood because of a setback or overextend yourself, ending your day on a high note is better than going to bed angry and ruminating on all your mistakes. This is not to say that if you fail, you should punish yourself with 50 lashes or an ice cold shower. Instead of a bubble bath, take a standard shower; instead of watching three episodes of Frasier, watch one. You should still maintain your routine, but that's all it will be.

Rewards can be a tricky thing, however. You need to have some level of discipline for them to work. If you make treating yourself to ice cream a reward, and you get it regardless of whether or not you succeeded, then it's not really a reward. There is also timing to consider, as a reward is technically an interruption if not timed right. The Pomodoro method is a standard method for increasing productivity by working in five-minute breaks to use how you see fit after 25 minutes (Boogaard, 2018). However, if you have trouble switching tasks, you may get stuck in the reward stage and permanently distracted.

You may have tried this in the past, as it is such a ubiquitous piece of advice, only to have it blow up in your face. You might not be wired for this technique, and that's perfectly alright. If you are the type that prefers to get all your work done in a long stretch, go for it!

Key Takeaways

- Seeking genuine self-improvement can have a transition process.

- While excitement is fuel, it can also lead to impulsive decisions that you will pay for later.

- Getting out of our comfort zone exposes us to the possibility of failure, which is terrifying. It is better to dip a toe in than not go in at all.

- Lists are a great way to plan and checking off items gives us a rush of motivation.

- Growing pains can create doubt; you can use autosuggestion to convince your subconscious that the idea of you failing is absurd.

- To stay on track, you need to limit interruptions and distractions wherever you can. This includes having to look for something, getting hungry, or acting on an idea out of fear of forgetting it. Prepare for these situations so you stay in the zone.

- Reward yourself for doing what you set out to do, but do not punish yourself for falling short. Our lives are supposed to improve from all this effort.

STAYING MOTIVATED AND ACCOUNTABLE

"You're going to mess up. So instead of trying to be perfect, learn how to be accountable."

- WHITNEY GOODMAN

You have learned a lot about not letting that little bug in your brain hold you back from everything you want to be. Your mind might be quieter, more focused, and kinder to you. You may have even taken the jump and started something you have been putting off for years. Still, there will come a time when this is not just a new part of your life, the novelty will wear off, and you will come to a fork in the road. It will either become a habit or you become complacent. You cannot power yourself into engagement; this makes the process torturous and isolating, which goes against the whole point of self-improvement. You need motivators that keep you going when things get rough or, more dangerously, monotonous.

The Art of Accountability

To keep you slightly on your toes, you should start looping people into your journey. Yes, showing off is always satisfying, but recall that we value the opinions of others over our own, sometimes to our own detriment. We can turn this around and use it to boost our own morale. That validation might get you excited to try to make a gift or help the other person with the new skills you have learned. The other side of the coin is that at the next family reunion, someone can ask, "Hey, are you still doing that thing?" You don't want the answer to be a sheepish *no*. While quitting something because it wasn't a good fit is valid, sometimes we just take our progress for granted and fall off the horse. The only thing at stake here is your pride, but it might be enough to keep you going.

A loved one might want to take up a similar endeavor. If there is one thing humans love more than sharing, it's teaching. You will be inspired to learn more yourself, have an answer to their questions, and better yet, gain a new perspective on your passion. Accountability can be a charged word and while there is an inherent risk, you can also think of it as being accountable for your success.

Seeking a Mentor

Once you are serious about your goals, it might be a good idea to seek out a mentor. A good mentor can give you a peek into the inner world you wish to be a part of. Whether it is a career, passion project, or fitness goal, talking to someone who has made the journey is inspiring. Having to give updates to a person you admire is also a great source of accountability and gives you more concrete timelines. There are a few routes you can go. You can go the paid route with a coach or a mentorship service. Since these services are advertised, you will likely get a response. Then there is your traditional mentoring where you find someone on your own and ask for their guidance. This is a more informal relationship, not one of a client and a service provider.

You need to consider what you hope the mentor-mentee relationship will be like and tailor your expectations accordingly. You might ask yourself why anyone would take on a mentee if they are not getting paid. For one, people like helping others, and the idea of a fresh face seeking their counsel is exceptionally satisfying. Their hard work has become legitimized when they are called on to teach. Also, mentees can become helping hands in the mentor's network. While you might not end up working directly under your mentor as you would in an academic setting, you should aim to become proficient enough to help if opportunity knocks.

Before you seek out a mentor, you should have an overall vision for your goals. Decide how often you want to see this person. You can do check-ins once a month where you ask for feedback or get more hands-on training (this falls into personal coaching and will most likely cost money).

You want to avoid picking a mentor in a different niche than you aim for. You would not ask an expert in calisthenics to train you how to lift heavy or ask a watercolors expert to show you how to oil paint. You need to be able to look at them and say to yourself, "I want to be that in a few years". You should know the lingo and have a basic understanding of the field. Your time with your mentor is valuable, and you want to avoid spending time on things you can figure out with a basic web search.

There are several ways to seek out mentors the old-fashioned way. Some good face time at a conference, talk, or networking event is always great. These are professional gatherings, so coming up and asking for advice is expected. See if your area of interest has classes online or in your area. You will meet like-minded people who have had success acquiring a mentor and you can even ask the instructor for advice. One way to break the ice at a public session is to ask a question in private after. You will have fewer eyes on you and more time to formulate deep questions. A potential mentor will seek curiosity, insight, and a desire to push the envelope.

Without in-person events, the internet will be both your best friend and worst enemy. So many experts have multiple professional profiles on every networking website under the sun. Cold emailing can be nerve-wracking; the mentor you are courting might be incredibly busy or have an unforgiving spam folder. Do not take it personally; just cast a wider net. Contact information is everywhere. While LinkedIn might gatekeep email addresses, plenty of companies and institutions have a point of contact you can use. Draft an email explaining what you are seeking, why you are interested in the subject, the work you have done so far, and why you specifically chose to approach this person as a mentor. Do they have an engaging teaching style? Is their work cutting-edge? Are they in a particular niche? If this person has an active social media presence, that can also be huge. Don't be afraid to like their posts, comment and ask questions, and use private messages. Keep your email brief and do not gush too much, as that can be off-putting. Schedule a follow-up video call where you can present more of your background and motivations. Think of this as a job interview and treat it as such.

Boundaries and effective communication are essential to ensuring you get the most from your partnership. Ultimately, this needs to be a professional relationship. A mentor should not see you as a burden. They should be on time for meetings and overall positive. While television may glorify the strict mentor character (Gregory House, Perry Cox etc.) who insults his mentee in the name of toughening them up, this will just destroy your confidence. The second you start dreading your meetings, especially if you have done everything you could to make progress, it is time to cut ties.

Another red flag you should look for is a mentor taking credit for your work. Just because they are helping you bring your vision to life does not mean they own it. While sharing the credit is perfectly acceptable, you should be working on projects that can showcase your talent to others, even if it is a passion project. A mentor should also keep their guidance and opinions professional. You should be wary if they gossip or badmouth others in the field to you or a colleague.

A mentor should also be willing to share tips and contacts with you. Sure, they can't give out proprietary information, but a mentor should be glad to help you grow your network and knowledge. If they are too cagey with their data, you will be stifled in your progress. While you may be excited to work with someone you admire, remember your boundaries. You should not come off as a superfan, you can show your enthusiasm by wanting to build off your research.

A good mentorship can look different depending on what your expectations are. Meetings don't need to occur often, but they should be consistent. Blocking out an hour once a month where you both have each other's full attention is crucial. You should leave these meetings charged up and excited to put their feedback into action. Neither of you should be dominating the hour. You should be allowed to describe your process and problems and ask questions without the mentor talking about themselves the entire time. Vulnerability is an asset to a mentor since it lets them share their past mistakes so that you can learn from them and avoid them on your own journey.

The mentee should show up prepared to every meeting. If you don't feel prepared enough, postpone your appointments until you have something to show. No one likes wasting their time; a cancellation is better than an awkward, wasted hour. You have to sense improvement with your mentor. As your understanding grows, you may notice that the quality of your questions will improve and that you are contributing more advanced ideas.

Fighting The Old You

You may be in a great place, but there is always a part of you that will miss your old life. It was familiar and comfortable, and when the chips are down or you get bored, it is easy to return to. No journey is linear, there will be points where you will be filled with doubt and wonder why you thought of doing something so ridiculous. Once change occurs, staying there is not a passive process, it will require some effort to maintain it for the rest of your life. All this effort is undoubtedly worth it in the end, even if there are times when you can't see it.

You may not be getting complacent in your passion project or new lifestyle, but you might be letting other things such as friends or cleanliness go. You cannot use time management as an excuse to backslide in other parts of your life. Remember your mantras and how to look at things objectively. Your laptop might need charging, but the cable is in another room. It will take one minute to fetch it so you are prepared to get right to work tomorrow. Be sure to incorporate time for cleaning up your workstation and taking care of your tools into your schedule. Life gives you enough resistance, don't become your own worst enemy. It's better to shave off a few minutes at the end of your day to set yourself up for success than walking up to your workstation the next day and feeling like it isn't worth it. Take pride in your space and it will take care of you.

Fueling Your Motivation

To keep your momentum going, you need to figure out ways to continue to inspire yourself. When we are engaged in a project for a long time, we sometimes lose sight as to what our end goal was and where we started. Keeping progress photos or old projects to flip through is vital (Millard, 2019). Progress can be slow and like a frog in a pot of slowly boiling water, we might not notice changes. Look at these points in your journey with kind eyes and pride. That previous version of you may have written some cringey poetry or played the worst rendition of *Wonderwall* on the guitar the world has ever had the misfortune of hearing, but that person was brave enough to shake it off and keep going.

If you are feeling particularly down or find yourself breaking all the good habits you have created, you might need to get a bit creative with your motivators. Visualize yourself after you have completed the task. Visualize how proud you will be when you complete your next project, how good it will feel for your grandma to praise you and take the helm as her favorite grandchild. Use your senses; think about how satisfying a hot shower is after a workout or hearing the laughter after your first standup performance (Baumgartner, 2011).

Using Your New Tools to Deal with Failure

I didn't hear no bell.

- Randy Marsh, South Park

We could talk about several historical underdog stories where the victor was clearly outmatched and only won the day through grit and smarts. Instead, let's look at something that is low stakes but can draw the ire of a considerable portion of the population—video games. In 2018, the gaming community was waiting on pins and needles for a game called *No Man's Sky*. The lead developer, Sean Murray, had been making the media rounds giving the public sneak peeks that they could sink their teeth into. He wasn't just talking to gaming journalists, he had to go on the Tonight Show with Stephen Colbert. It promised to be a game where the player, bound by the constraints of astrophysics, could hop around the universe on ships they built and stocked and go on adventures with their online friends. It was an ambitious project, but the hype and press led them to get a huge marketing push from Sony and a triple-A label. Despite all this, what would follow would be one of the most infamous releases in gaming history.

When the game dropped, it was revealed to be a buggy unplayable mess. The mechanics were repetitive and there was no concrete goal or story to grasp. Entire features that were expected were just not there; the game was not even playable online. So what happened? How could a game with so much promise choke so hard at the finish line? It didn't; the game was doomed from the start.

Triple-A games typically have hundreds of people working on them with a ton of resources. *No Man's Sky* had a team of 15 people. Sony may have given them a marketing push, but that was it. Sean Murray, a shy video game tech nerd, had to manage the press, go on interviews, all while running his own indie development company. He was under a ton of pressure made worse by the fact that Sony chained them to a deadline they would never make and set expectations that were rightfully skewed by the $60 price tag . After all that work, all Sean had to show for it was a hack job of a game. He was personally dragged online and even received death threats. The gaming community felt duped, and by Sean personally.

Sean was at a crossroads; he could either pocket the money that he made from the insane pre order sales, be shunned by everyone he ever admired, and become synonymous with failure, or pick himself up and do what he initially set out to do.

Sean had to regroup if he had any hope of salvaging the game and his future in the gaming industry. There was no room for a pity party. While Sean objectively failed everyone, he could not consider himself a failure, or else he would never dig his way out of this hole.

Sean rose to the occasion as a leader. He knew he had to focus and despite literal rocks being hurled his way, he did not give into the temptation to justify, deflect, or worst of all, lash out. Sean told his team to not give the press any information and just get to work. He told his team to stop doomscrolling through the bad press and focus on fixing the game.

He alone took the burden of that information and made it into data that he could use to prioritize where to start fixing things. One by one, he released patches (for free, by the way) that not only repaired the game but made it better than anyone could ever have dreamed of. Through all this, he remained charitable to the community that shunned him by adding all new free features, instead of hiding them behind paywalls and lootboxes like other companies.

Sean and his small team took what looked like a hopeless situation and turned everything around, breaking records and winning awards left, right, and center. All because failure was not an option (Woog, n.d.).

You may come to a point where you consider yourself a failure. Maybe you stopped practicing for months on end, bombed at a public showing, or regressed in your health. Whatever the situation, this is a vulnerable time. It might seem that the universe has decided to confirm your fears, that the old you is all you are and all you ever will be. Here's the thing, coming up short, even repeatedly, does not make you a failure so long as you learn something, pick yourself up, and try again. You need to be able to deal with setbacks and not let your mind run with the idea that taking a risk was never worth it. That inner voice that is trying to keep you in a cage will come back stronger than ever.

Do not be afraid to lean on others. Everyone can relate to hard times and disappointment. They can shine some much needed perspective on your own situation through the lens of a person who could never see you as a loser.

Learning to take setbacks in your stride is a valuable skill. Humor is your best ally here. If you trip on the sidewalk, people might remember it more if you walked away pouting or angry at the fact that you just embarrassed yourself. However, if you laughed and made a jab at your own expense, they will remember that you were funny, even in an awkward situation. That is an admirable quality. It also serves to minimize setbacks in your head. While this would normally be a bad thing, you might be a person who blows up every botch into something catastrophic. You effectively swung your mind in the other direction and landed in a neutral area. The darkness of the human soul detests mockery, laughs your misfortune into submission, and keeps moving forward.

Key Takeaways

- Stay accountable! One of the biggest keys to taking real control of your life is learning to stay accountable for your actions.

- We all slip up from time to time. This doesn't mean that you should beat yourself up about it. Instead, if you do notice yourself slipping back into your hold habits, use the new you to push the old you away. The more you do this, the stronger your new habits become.

- Keep fueling your motivation. Keep your forward momentum going by reminding yourself where you started, how far you've come, and where you want to end up.

- Do yourself a big favor and seek out a mentor!

CONCLUSION

Mental clutter and negativity may have once stopped you from achieving your goals, but no more! By gaining perspective, keeping a positive attitude, and rewiring your brain, you can stop rumination dead in its tracks. No one will blame you for finding this process intimidating. Our worries have been a security blanket for our whole lives, and we might think of ourselves as naive for abandoning it. We let our own cynicism and the opinions of others dictate how we live and perceive both ourselves and the world. We are so set in our ways that we become resistant to the notion that there is another way to live.

You have so many tools now, from the knowledge of how to properly examine the source of a negative thought pattern, exercises to help you focus and to relax, to a new way to organize your mental and physical world. With these things in place, you might have a new drive to try

CONCLUSION

something new. This lease on life can be addictive, but you can backslide if you don't keep your feet on the ground in regard to progress or perceived shortcomings. Through therapy, trusted friends, and our new resourcefulness we can reach new heights and make them permanent. You should be your own biggest advocate and own your goals and your success.

Thank You for Reading

While you're here, **may I ask you the small favor to leave a quick review or rating?**

Even though the simple act of leaving a review will take you **less than a minute**, it will give a huge amount of support, and as an independent author **I appreciate the gift of your time more than you know**!

To make it quick and easy, when you scan one of the QR codes below it will take you directly to your Amazon review page.

Amazon Review US　　　　**Amazon Review UK**

Thank you for your help and support.

Best Wishes,

- Lucas

Remember that you can download your 3 free gifts by scanning the QR code at the beginning of the book.

REFERENCES

ACT vs. CBT: What's the difference? (2022, April 15). Psych Central. https://psychcentral.com/lib/whats-the-difference-between-acceptance-and-commitment-therapy-mindfulness-based-cognitive-therapy

Bault, N., Joffily, M., Rustichini, A., & Coricelli, G. (2011). Medial prefrontal cortex and striatum mediate the influence of social comparison on the decision process. *Proceedings of the National Academy of Sciences, 108*(38),

16044–16049. https://doi.org/10.1073/pnas.1100892108

Baumgartner. (2011). *Visualize It | Psychology Today*. https://www.psychologytoday.com/intl/blog/the-psychology-dress/201111/visualize-it

Bhandari, S. (2021). *Stress Symptoms: Effects of Stress on the Body*. WebMD. https://www.webmd.com/balance/stress-management/stress-symptoms-effects_of-stress-on-the-body

Blue light has a dark side. (2012, May 1). Harvard Health. https://www.health.harvard.edu/staying-healthy/blue-light-has-a-dark-side

Boogaard, K. B. (2018, January 18). *I Hate Productivity Hacks, Except for This One*. The Muse. https://www.themuse.com/advice/take-it-from-someone-who-hates-productivity-

REFERENCES

hacksthe-pomodoro-technique-actually-works

Brewer, J. (2021). *Unwinding Anxiety: New science shows how to break the cycles of worry and fear to heal your mind.* New York: Avery, an imprint of Penguin Random House.

Carucci, A. (2022, August 22). *All-or-Nothing Thinking: Examples, Effects, and How to Manage.* Psych Central. https://psychcentral.com/health/all-or-nothing-thinking-examples

Cascio, C. N., O'Donnell, M. B., Tinney, F. J., Lieberman, M. D., Taylor, S. E., Strecher, V. J., & Falk, E. B. (2016). Self-affirmation activates brain systems associated with self-related processing and reward and is reinforced by future orientation. *Social Cognitive and Affective Neuroscience, 11*(4), 621–629. https://doi.org/10.1093/scan/nsv136

Cootey, D. (2019, June 14). *ADHD Humor: My Gift and My Curse.* https://www.additudemag.com/adhd-humor-gift-and-curse/

Coue, E. (1920). *Self Mastery Through Conscious Autosuggestion, by Emile Coué.* The Project Gutenberg. https://www.gutenberg.org/files/27203/27203-h/27203-h.htm

Cuzzone, K. (2020, September 12). *Fortune Telling Is the Toxic Habit You Need to Break.* PureWow. https://www.purewow.com/wellness/fortune-telling-thoughts

Do Affirmations Work? Yes, but There's a Catch. (2020, September 1). Healthline. https://www.healthline.com/health/mental-health/do-affirmations-work

Fletcher, J. (2022, April 22). *Catastrophizing: What Is*

REFERENCES

It and How to Stop. Psych Central. https://psychcentral.com/lib/what-is-catastrophizing

Flynn, C. (2020, March 26). Therapy by Phone or Video Chat Kinda Sucks. Here's How to Make It Better. *Vice*. https://www.vice.com/en/article/xgqped/video-phone-therapy-coronavirus-quarantine

Gawande, A. (2011). *The Checklist Manifesto: How to Get Things Right*. Picador;

Gomez, I. B. (2022). *What Is Magical Thinking? Effects of Cognitive Distortion*. GoodRx. https://www.goodrx.com/health-topic/mental-health/magical-thinking-effects-cognitive-distortion

Griffith, M. (2020, July 29). *How 'Junebugging' Can Change the Way You Clean With ADHD*. The Mighty.

https://themighty.com/topic/adhd/cleaning-method-adhd-hate-chores/

How Long Does it Take to Recover From Burnout? (n.d.). Retrieved March 23, 2023, from https://www.wellics.com/blog/how-long-to-recover-from-burnout

Joy, R. (2022, August 31). *Cognitive Distortions: 10 Examples of Distorted Thinking.* Healthline. https://www.healthline.com/health/cognitive-distortions

Kim, J., Kwon, J. H., Kim, J., Kim, E. J., Kim, H. E., Kyeong, S., & Kim, J.-J. (2021). The effects of positive or negative self-talk on the alteration of brain functional connectivity by performing cognitive tasks. *Scientific Reports, 11*(1), Article 1. https://doi.org/10.1038/s41598-021-94328-9

Kleiven, G. S., Hjeltnes, A., Råbu, M., & Moltu, C. (2020). Opening Up: Clients' Inner Struggles in the Initial Phase of Therapy. *Frontiers in Psychology, 11*, 591146. https://doi.org/10.3389/fpsyg.2020.591146

Kondo, M. (2014). *The life-changing magic of tidying up: The Japanese art of decluttering and organizing*. Ten Speed Press.

Kubala, K. (2022, May 27). *ADHD and Disrespectful Behavior: A Symptom or Rudeness?* Psych Central. https://psychcentral.com/adhd/adhd-and-disrespectful-behavior

Ludwig, P. (n.d.). *Why Does a "To-Do Today" List Work? | Procrastination.com*. Retrieved February 20, 2023, from https://procrastination.com/blog/25/why-does-a-to-do-today-list-work

Martin, G. (n.d.). *'The road to hell is paved with good intentions'—The meaning and origin of this phrase*. Phrasefinder. Retrieved February 20,

2023, from
https://www.phrases.org.uk/meanings/the-road-to-hell-is-paved-with-good-intentions.html

Mcleod, S. (2022, November 3). *Asch Conformity Line Experiment.* https://simplypsychology.org/asch-conformity.html

Michael, V. (2022, July 30). *Understanding Overgeneralization: A Cognitive Distortion.* Mental Health Center Kids. https://mentalhealthcenterkids.com/blogs/articles/overgeneralization

Millard, E. (2019, January 6). 5 Ways to Use Before-and-After Photos to Motivate | Weight Loss | MyFitnessPal. *MyFitnessPal Blog.* https://blog.myfitnesspal.com/5-ways-to-use-before-and-after-photos-to-motivate/

REFERENCES

Nast, C. (2022, November 15). *Prince Charles and Princess Diana's Tortured Relationship*. Vanity Fair. https://www.vanityfair.com/style/2022/11/prince-charles-diana-relationship

National Institute for Mental Health. (n.d.). *Panic Disorder: When Fear Overwhelms*. National Institute of Mental Health (NIMH). Retrieved March 30, 2023, from https://www.nimh.nih.gov/health/publications/panic-disorder-when-fear-overwhelms

Palma, M. (2021, September 10). Discounting the Positive | A Corroding Cognitive Distortion. *Adam Fout*. https://adamfout.com/discounting-the-positive/

Rapee, R. M., & Heimberg, R. G. (1997). A cognitive-behavioral model of anxiety in social phobia.

Behaviour Research and Therapy, 35(8), 741–756. https://doi.org/10.1016/S0005-7967(97)00022-3

Russo, C., Danioni, F., Zagrean, I., & Barni, D. (2022). Changing Personal Values through Value-Manipulation Tasks: A Systematic Literature Review Based on Schwartz's Theory of Basic Human Values. *European Journal of Investigation in Health, Psychology and Education, 12*(7), 692–715. https://doi.org/10.3390/ejihpe12070052

Salehinejad, M. A., Ghanavati, E., Rashid, M. H. A., & Nitsche, M. A. (2021). Hot and cold executive functions in the brain: A prefrontal-cingular network. *Brain and Neuroscience Advances, 5*, 23982128211007770. https://doi.org/10.1177/23982128211007769

Sedgwick, J. A., Merwood, A., & Asherson, P. (2019).

REFERENCES

The positive aspects of attention deficit hyperactivity disorder: A qualitative investigation of successful adults with ADHD. *ADHD Attention Deficit and Hyperactivity Disorders, 11*(3), 241–253. https://doi.org/10.1007/s12402-018-0277-6

Segal, J. (2023). *Coping with a Breakup or Divorce—HelpGuide.org*. Https://Www.Helpguide.Org. https://www.helpguide.org/articles/grief/dealing-with-a-breakup-or-divorce.htm

Star, K. (n.d.-a). *Cognitive Distortions: What Is Magnification and Minimization?* Verywell Mind. Retrieved March 30, 2023, from https://www.verywellmind.com/magnification-and-minimization-2584183

Star, K. (n.d.-b). *How the Word "Should" Can Increase Your Anxiety*. Verywell Mind. Retrieved March 30, 2023, from https://www.verywellmind.com/should-statements-2584193

Steiner, S. (n.d.). *The 5 Things People Regret Most On Their Deathbed.* Business Insider. Retrieved February 7, 2023, from https://www.businessinsider.com/5-things-people-regret-on-their-deathbed-2013-12

Sweeney, S. (n.d.). *Auto Suggestion Techniques to Help You Change Your Life.* Online Hypnotherapy Clinic. Retrieved March 24, 2023, from https://www.onlinehypnotherapyclinic.com/auto-suggestion-techniques.html

The 54321 Grounding Technique For Anxiety. (2020, June 29). *Insight Timer Blog.* https://insighttimer.com/blog/54321-grounding-technique/

The Eisenhower Matrix: Introduction & 3-Minute Video Tutorial. (2017, February 7).

REFERENCES

https://www.eisenhower.me/eisenhower-matrix/

The Science of Feng Shui. (n.d.). Retrieved February 21, 2023, from https://www.millerhomes.co.uk/blog/2020/may/the-science-of-feng-shui.aspx

Thompson, M. (2020, March 9). *According to Warren Buffett, Honing This One Skill Can Improve Your Worth by 50 Percent.* Medium. https://entrepreneurshandbook.co/according-to-warren-buffett-honing-this-one-skill-can-improve-your-worth-by-50-percent-9221cd79356

Time Management and ADHD: Day Planners. (n.d.). *CHADD.* Retrieved February 20, 2023, from https://chadd.org/for-adults/time-management-planner/

Why is task switching so hard? (n.d.). ADDept.

Retrieved March 21, 2023, from https://www.addept.org/living-with-adult-add-adhd/task-switching

Wilson, T. (2018, March 28). *How to do a Candle Gazing Meditation (Trataka)*. Awake & Mindful. https://awakeandmindful.com/how-to-do-a-candle-gazing-meditation-trataka/

Wise, N. (2017). *The Pros and Cons of Putting Your Bills on Auto-Pay*. Northwestern Mutual. https://www.northwesternmutual.com/life-and-money/the-pros-and-cons-of-putting-your-bills-on-auto-pay/

Woog, B. (n.d.). *Looking At How Far No Man's Sky Has Come*. Game Informer. Retrieved March 29, 2023, from https://www.gameinformer.com/2019/07/15/looking-at-how-far-no-mans-sky-has-come

Yeo, L. B. (2021). Psychological And Physiological

REFERENCES

Benefits Of Plants In The Indoor Environment: A Mini And In-Depth Review. *International Journal of Built Environment and Sustainability*, 8(1), Article 1. https://doi.org/10.11113/ijbes.v8.n1.597

Printed in Great Britain
by Amazon